"Though the subject is mother loss, _____
living a life of improvement. *MOM'S GONE, NOW WHAT?*
covers the topic of mother loss clearly and practically while
simultaneously being a book about living the observed life—
it is much larger than its page count. As an English major,
I know that great books have stories that are well told and
an additional element that rises to the level of what I refer
to as 'eternal truth.' That truth has the potential to make us
better humans. *MOM'S GONE, NOW WHAT?* has that."

—MITCHELL BRUSKI
CEO (ret.) Kenneth Young Centers,
Community mental health center

"If you've suffered mother loss, no matter your age or the
reason, *MOM'S GONE, NOW WHAT?* is the book to read.
You'll find a story you can identify with, as I did in the tales
of three women who experienced the loss of their mother
from dementia. Amy, Jen, and Carrie's stories enlighten the
reader and contain helpful advice for current caregivers."

—SHIRLEY WOOLAWAY
Author of *Dementia: Up Close and Personal, A Caregiver's Tale*

"I love the manner in which the author organized *MOM'S
GONE, NOW WHAT?*—how she integrated the interviews
along with her commentary and ends each chapter with a
homework assignment. *MOM'S GONE, NOW WHAT?* is
a forthright, revealing, intimate book. It's almost as if the
reader is sitting across the table from the author as she shares
her story and the stories of others. What a marvelous book!"

—ROBERT ALSTON
CEO (ret.) Friendship Senior Options,
Senior living communities

PRAISE FOR
MOM'S GONE, NOW WHAT?
(Continued)

MOM'S GONE, NOW WHAT? is more interesting than most novels with its personal stories of overcoming loss; contains more wisdom than most philosophy books; is more heartwarming than positive mental attitude books; is more spiritually uplifting than most spiritual books. Reading this book is like finding a sisterhood and spending time with a wise, caring friend.

—PAULINE HAYTON
Author of nine books including,
If You Love Me, Kill Me—An Eldercare Story

Not many people are able to fully grasp or articulate the complex and profound impact of the mother-daughter relationship. Mershon truly understands the immeasurable loss and the power it has to completely redefine us. This book is essential to help guide women through a process that can be as messy and overwhelming as swimming through glue. Kudos to Mershon for tackling this painful and sometimes taboo social topic with honesty, clarity, and sound advice.

—ILANA TOLPIN LEVITT
Author of *What's Mom Still Got to do With It? Breathe new life into your career by understanding your mother-daughter relationship*

Mom's Gone, Now What?
Copyright © 2020 by Mershon Niesner

Cover and interior designed by Lance Buckley.
www.lancebuckley.com

ISBN: 978-0-9743076-1-9

For more information on quantity sales, how to schedule author events, use of quotes, and an ongoing supportive blog visit: www.mershonniesner.com

Publisher's Cataloging-In-Publication Data
(Prepared by The Donohue Group, Inc.)

Names: Niesner, Mershon, author.
Title: Mom's Gone, Now What? : Ten Steps to Help Daughters Move Forward After Mother Loss / Mershon Niesner.
Description: [Marco Island, Florida] : [The Bell Group], [2020] | Includes bibliographical references.
Identifiers: ISBN 9780974307619 (paperback) | ISBN 9780974307626 (ebook)
Subjects: LCSH: Mothers--Death--Psychological aspects. | Mothers and daughters. | Bereavement--Psychological aspects. | Conduct of life. | Niesner, Mershon--Family.
Classification: LCC BF575.G7 N54 2020 (print)
| LCC BF575.G7 (ebook) | DDC 155.9/370854--dc23

Mom's Gone, NOW WHAT?

TEN STEPS TO
HELP DAUGHTERS
MOVE FORWARD
AFTER MOTHER LOSS

Mershon Niesner

PREFACE

*The most beautiful people we have known
are those who have known defeat, known
suffering, known struggle, known loss, and
have found their way out of those depths.*

—Elisabeth Kübler-Ross, author of *On Death And Dying*

You're holding *Mom's Gone, Now What?* for a reason. Perhaps you've recently experienced mother loss and are wondering, "now what?" as you struggle to move forward. Maybe the initial sting of loss is behind you and you're ready to affirm your progress or find comfort and camaraderie with women who have had experiences similar to yours. This book can meet you where you are and help you move forward to where you want to go in your mother loss journey.

Perhaps you're reading this book to learn how to cope with loss on behalf of a granddaughter or other relative who needs your support. Maybe you're a member of the Silent Generation, born between 1925-1945, and planning for your final years. This book offers tips on how to help your family cope with life after you're gone. If you, or someone you love, are in the early stages of Alzheimer's, *Mom's Gone, Now What?* can be a conversation starter concerning care options, resources, and steps to help loved ones cope with what's to come.

Whatever your reasons for reading, welcome. Welcome to a circle of women who have lost or are losing their mothers and those who care about these daughters.

I wrote this book to acknowledge you and, with the help of others, coach you through your journey of loss. Although I too am acquainted with mother loss—my mother died when I was eight and her mother died when my mother was three—I can't know exactly how you feel. If nothing else, writing this book taught me that each loss and journey forward is different. To address the unique nature of loss, *Mom's Gone, Now What?* shares stories of loss and strength from a variety of perspectives.

Writing this book was a spiritual calling for me. It started with a nudge from Virginia, a ninety-one-year-old woman I met for the first time on a warm, sunny day in the middle of my street. I saw her talking to workmen about a vacant lot she owned across from my house. I approached her and introduced myself. Two hours later, after she learned I had writing experience, she encouraged me to join a local writers' group and insisted that I write a book. It was spring, a time for planting. Virginia turned over the soil of my life and planted the seed for this endeavor.

Soon after meeting Virginia, I knew the topic for my book. I'd worked on a variety of life issues, including mother loss, for eight years in group therapy, participated in two motherless daughters groups, had written topic-related poetry and letters. Mother loss had taken up much real estate in my psyche over the years. Now was the time to write a book about it.

I started my process by interviewing over fifty daughters from a variety of cultural backgrounds and ranging in age from eighteen to eighty-three. Some, like myself, experienced early loss, others were abandoned. Two daughters lost mothers to homicide. Some lost their mothers twice to Alzheimer's, once as their memory faded, then again to a physical death. One woman's mother was physically present but inattentive. Whatever your experience, these stories can speak to you.

I started writing this book from the egocentric perspective of my own journey. I wanted to relate how happy my child-hood was and how I had thrived during nearly seven decades of living without a mother. Then I woke up and realized my story was limited. I'm still a work-in-progress and not every-thing has gone as smoothly as I'd like to imagine. After all these years, I still struggle with abandonment, intimacy, and confrontation issues. In speaking with other daughters, I too benefited from what they had learned, how they coped, how they felt, and how they answered the "Now What?" question.

I interviewed women over the phone, via email, and in person over a cup of coffee or pot of tea. I chose them, or they chose me, because of our ties to mother loss. Some early loss daughters learned of my project from Gale, a therapist who emailed members of her Motherless Daughters Groups. Daughters also came to me by way of friends, Facebook groups, and blogs. As painful as telling her story often was, each daughter wanted to share her experience in order to help another. They believed that becoming a part of this book would give greater meaning to their loss. Not every story I heard is used in this book, however, every story contributed to the narrative.

Some daughters said it was the first time they had shared the details of their stories. Others acknowledged that they hadn't thought about their mother's death or abandonment in many years. Discussing mother memories brought up a variety of feelings depending on the relationship, the type of loss, and the length of time since their mother loss experience. Mother conversations were painful, joyful, nostalgic, upsetting and—nearly always—healing.

The ten steps suggested in this book are not the only ways to find healing after loss. They are simply the steps that bubbled up as helpful and meaningful when I examined my own history and talked with daughters. The steps are not lineal—one step doesn't lead to the next. Some steps may not apply to you at all. If this is the case, skip the step and continue to the next. Jump around and see what resonates with you.

Writing isn't foreign to me. As a child welfare social worker in the late '60s in rural Georgia, writing was frequently part of my job. In addition to abuse and neglect cases, I interviewed prospective adoptive parents, wrote their case histories, and supervised their adoptions. I also worked with unwed mothers, wrote their stories, and placed their babies with adoptive parents. This was a challenging career for a twenty-one year old right out of college. Perhaps because I was young, inexperienced, and lacked the emotional ties motherhood brings, I was able to cope with the drama that came with moving abused children into foster care or holding a teenage mother's hand prior to signing the release for her baby to be placed for adoption. These experiences added to my knowledge of mother/daughter relationships.

Years later, after seeing my own children into their school-age years, I owned a marketing/communications business where I wrote newsletters, press releases, video scripts, and brochures. In my most recent career, I was a Certified Personal/Professional Coach. As a Life Coach, I worked primarily with women to help them succeed in their personal and professional lives by helping them set goals that reflected their values while holding them accountable to what they wanted to do and affirming their progress as they worked toward achieving their hopes and dreams. I bring this coaching experience to you as a "coach between the pages," asking coaching questions at the end of each step to help you move forward in your "Now What?" process.

As the Chair of the Board of Directors for a community mental health center and, later, Board Chair of a continuing care, senior living organization, I also bring the heart for, and expertise in, the fields of mental health and elder care.

I've been without a mother for over sixty-five years and I'm at peace with my early loss. This is not to say that my loss doesn't continue to impact my life. In addition to the traits I mentioned earlier, I still expect people to precede me in death. Having an orderly, organized life helps me feel more in control because I know for sure that bad things can happen unexpectedly. I love to see my daughters "mother" their children as it reminds me of how my mother might have mothered me.

I often think of Wendy, Helen, Marti, Roni, Vicki and the many other daughters I interviewed for this book and wonder how they are doing. In my mind, they stood behind me as I wrote and kept me motivated to see this project through to publication so their stories could be read by others. I will hold them in my heart forever. Now, dear reader, although I may never meet you or hear your story, I will think of you as you join us on this journey. I pray this book will help you to feel less alone as you find your way.

Mershon Niesner
Marco Island, Florida
June 2020

STEP ONE

SHARE YOUR STORY

*My mother memories that are closest to my heart are
the small gentle ones that I have carried over from
the days of my childhood. They are not profound,
but they have stayed with me through life, and
when I am very old, they will still be near.*

—Margaret Sanger, American nurse and activist

The willingness to share our story signals a desire to leave a
legacy and to turn pain into a message of hope for others.
This is why Step One is important. As you read daughters'
stories, you may find memories of your own rising to the
surface. If this happens, consider writing them down or
sharing your thoughts with someone you trust.

My Early Loss Story

It was a late afternoon in April 1954, when my life as a
regular eight-year-old began to unravel. I was in my bedroom, which had a twin bed pushed up against the wall,
two windows with Venetian blinds—the kind that if I lifted
one of the slats at night I feared I'd see an imaginary eye
looking back at me—a dresser, and a student desk. The

best part about my room was the shelves above the scary windows where the imaginary, scary man could be lurking. My dad had installed them to hold my Storybook Doll collection including: Little Red Riding Hood, Cinderella, and a recently added Queen Elizabeth Coronation Doll.

Directly across the hall from my room, my parents were in the master bedroom talking quietly with my Aunt Lucy. From where I stood, I could see my dad, Leon, a handsome man with black hair, blue eyes, fair skin, and a masculine, stocky build. Next to him stood my tall, large-boned aunt. My mother, Winnifred—Winnie for short—lay on my parents' bed. Even from a distance, I could tell she wasn't smiling her beautiful smile, her brown eyes were dull, and her brown hair was messy. Although my mother was also tall, five feet nine inches, and large-boned like her sister, I was aware that she had lost weight. She seemed to be shrinking before my eyes.

My mother had recently returned from spending a few days in the local hospital, an old building downtown with a flashing pink, neon sign. What I didn't know at the time, was her leukemia diagnosis. Even if I had known, I would not have been equipped at age eight to understand the consequences of this dreaded disease. In those days, leukemia was nearly always fatal.

A few days earlier, I was surprised when my aunt arrived in Grand Island, Nebraska from Walnut Creek, California, where she lived alone in her post-war bungalow with her black cocker spaniel, Winnie-the-Pooh. I had seen pictures of her house and was looking forward to a trip to California and meeting her dog someday. Aunt Lucy, a registered nurse with a Master's Degree in Public Health, had taken a leave of absence from her job as a public health administrator and settled Winnie-the-Pooh with friends in order to travel to Nebraska and be with her sister.

Aunt Lucy was an experienced caregiver. In addition to her professional experience, she frequently cared for my mother when they were children. My mother was three, almost four, my aunt eight, and their oldest sister, Eugenia, thirteen, when their mother died of complications from a ruptured appendix. In retrospect, it seemed strange that Aunt Lucy took on a mother role since, as an adult, she had no children of her own.

According to my cousin, who heard stories from her mother Eugenia, our grandfather was immersed in his own grief and, as a physician, threw himself into his work leaving little time for his three daughters. Just as my Aunt Lucy took special interest in me after my mother died, another unmarried aunt cared for my mother and her sisters after my mother's mother died. Although this aunt was present in their lives, from what I know, it was Aunt Lucy who nurtured my mother. They were very close. Now, thirty years later, she stepped back into her familiar, big-sister-caregiver shoes.

In addition to my aunt, my mother had her capable, caring husband by her side. My dad had also taken leave from his job in hospital administration to watch over his wife's care.

As I lingered in my bedroom I heard the adults' conversation. It went like this:

"I think we should leave for Omaha tomorrow," my aunt said.

What? I thought. *They're leaving Grand Island?*

I couldn't figure out why they would be leaving Grand Island and I wondered what was going to happen to me?

Will I be left with strangers? How long will they be gone?

I was close to tears when Dad approached my room. To hide my emotions, I pretended to be looking under my bed for a lost red shoe. I wasn't much of a crier, not even when I skinned my knee. We weren't an outwardly emotional family. I would have been embarrassed to have my dad see me in tears and I wanted to show him that I was a big girl.

"Tomorrow we're taking your mother to a hospital in Omaha," my dad said in a gentle voice.

As I peered out from where I was kneeling beside the bed, fear kept my voice barely above a whisper when I asked, "Are you taking me with you?"

"Of course we're taking you," he said. As far as I can remember, that was the extent of our conversation. Perhaps my dad, consumed with his own anxiety, had not considered *my* fears. I don't recall talking about the things that scared us.

At that moment, further discussion didn't matter to me anyway because I was so relieved to know I wasn't going to be left behind. This was the first time I felt the fear associated with possible abandonment—it would not be my last.

The next morning, we climbed into Betsy, our blue Chevrolet sedan. My mother lay across the back seat, her head in her sister's lap. My dad and I were in the front seat. This was decades before seat belts or rules about where kids sat in cars. The trip was uneventful except I remember feeling worried about my mother being sick when I heard her asking Aunt Lu to open the back window because she was having trouble breathing.

My dad's best friend, Dr. Ken Brown, his wife, Peg, and their two daughters were our host family in Omaha. I was glad to be among loving people with whom I was acquainted and felt comfortable. The daughters were close to my age and we had been friends in Grand Island before they moved to Omaha.

In those days, not much could be done for leukemia—no chemo, no radiation—just blood transfusions and drugs. In fact, so much blood was required, our neighbors, friends, and family traveled the 150 miles to Omaha to donate blood in my mother's name.

Most afternoons I went to the hospital with my dad. My Mom, propped up on pillows, showed me where they had taken samples of bone marrow from her sternum. I know now they tested the bone marrow for red blood cells. All I saw then was a small incision under a gauze bandage, but I remember being frightened by the wound. It seemed to confirm the gravity of her illness.

During my visit, my mother gave me the little paper cups in which she received her pills. The cups were more precious to me than she knew because they helped me feel close to her when we were apart. Although not soft and cuddly, they were like beloved stuffed animals, something tangible to hold on to as I fell asleep. As I clutched one cup at bedtime, I kept the rest on my bedside table.

Normally, I bounded out of bed early in the morning. But on May 24, 1954, in the unfamiliar, sun-drenched bedroom of our friends' home, I burrowed under the covers. Intuition told me to stay in bed and delay the start of the day. I ignored the voices downstairs and the morning sounds coming through the window. As it grew late, my dad and aunt came to my bedroom.

As they approached from the stairs, I again sensed something was wrong. My dad looked tired and wrinkled, like he'd been up all night. His glasses almost hid his eyes but I could tell they were red-rimmed. My aunt hung back as my dad sat next to me on the bed.

"Your mother died last night," he said.

I had a hard time grasping the meaning of his words. Then, they hit me like a giant wave.

My mom was gone. Dead. I would never see her again.

I remember the three of us crying. My aunt stood just inside the room, while my dad held me in his arms. When the tears finally stopped, I felt weak and scared and tired. This was where my memories of how I felt ended.

The weeks and months following my mother's death are a blur, as if I fell down a rabbit hole. Therapists and others have questioned me about my feelings following her death but, no matter how hard I tried, how willing I was to confront my feelings, how prepared I was to go to a place of profound sadness, nothing surfaced and I must be faithful to the truth as I share my story.

Although it might not seem unusual for an eight-year-old to suppress her emotions, most daughters I spoke with who had experienced early loss clearly remembered their feelings the days and months following the death of their mothers.

One exception to this lapse is a memory from my mom's funeral. I clearly remember pink carnations adorning her closed casket. As a result of this visual memory, I feel a loving connection to my mother whenever I see pink carnations. I recently learned from the novel, *The Language of Flowers* by Vanessa Diffenbaugh, that pink carnations mean, "I will never forget you." Now these simple flowers have taken on even greater significance for me and I am grateful for this small memory.

Grief over losing a parent at a young age is about more than the memories of a child. Grief is also about dealing with loss for a lifetime. Though I lack clear memories of my emotional state as an eight-year-old, I have a lifetime of experience dealing with mother loss and I clearly remember the details of my journey in the years that followed.

I remember feeling sad and missing my mom when I was sick and when I became a mother myself. I remember feeling different and outside the circle of my friends who had mothers still living. I remember how not having a mother made me feel sad on Mother's Day and still does after all these years. But mostly I remember the joyful and fulfilling childhood I shared with my dad. We created a life that overcame tragedy and embraced abundant living. This I clearly remember.

Stories of Fathers and Last Words

As a teen and young adult, I took my dad for granted. I eventually came to realize, however, just how fortunate I was to have him in my life. We had no relatives close-by to take over a mothering role. It was just us—which turned out to be fine. When I was in my sixties, my dad revealed to me how frightened he was at the prospect of rearing a little girl alone. But during my childhood, he created a calm, confident atmosphere that provided the positive framework for me to move forward and thrive.

Prior to writing this book, I framed my mother's brief involvement in my life by her absence from it rather than by her presence and her mothering. Her absence meant I was the young lady who was embarrassed to talk to my dad, or anyone else, about bras, girdles, and menstruation. I was the child who avoided conversations about families, for fear I'd have to say, "My mom died." I was the sick kid at home alone on the couch all day while my only parent was at work. And I was the bundle-of-anxieties-kid when my dad was five minutes late returning home from work.

Although my dad used to say, "Your mom taught you manners and how to be a lady," I didn't give my mom enough credit for her contributions to my upbringing. I've only recently realized that, not only did she teach me to say "please" and "thank you," she also taught me to show respect to my teachers, friends, and family members. Later, my dad also emphasized the importance of respect but during my early years he was away much of the time—first serving in World War Two and later, Korea—so my early, formative training fell to my mother.

As I watched her place antique, hand-painted dishes on card tables in anticipation of her bridge club luncheon, she showed me how to be an attentive hostess, how to put the silverware in the right places, and how to honor and embrace female friends. Her death taught me that life can be short and the importance of living each day with zest. And, she demonstrated daily how a beautiful smile could brighten most everyone's day.

The morning I learned that my mother had died, my dad also shared with me her last words. He said, "Your mother's last words were that she hoped you will grow up to be a wonderful woman." These last words, as relayed by my father, are the one detail of her death I remember with precise clarity. They became a beacon of hope in my life.

My mom thought of me at the end. She loved me. I was special to her.

"Wonderful" can be interrupted in many ways, so I had a broad palette with which to fulfill my mother's last request. I started with the meaning, "Be a good girl." Children chisel behavior down to good and bad without nuance. Sixty-five years later, I define wonderful as a person who glorifies God by living life to the fullest, caring about others, and striving to leave the world better than I found it.

Although my mother's last words were significant to me, it never occurred to me that other daughters might also have a "last words" experience. Until I met Veronica.

"Veronica, like in the comics," she told me when we spoke on the phone, "but I prefer to be called Roni." Roni holds both masters and doctorate degrees in adult education and has expertise in life-long learning. At the time of our conversation Roni was sixty-nine years old and knew a thing or two about making life choices. She had spent time examining her past. Her dissertation, "Life is a Banquet: Who is Staying for Dessert and Why?" examines the factors that assist women to live with vibrance regardless of their age or health. As I talked with Roni, I felt her vigor and energy coming through the phone.

Not only did I feel a connection with Roni because of her delightful personality, we also bonded because the timeline of our mother loss was similar. Roni was nine when her mother died at the age of thirty-four. The similarities of our mother loss experience, however, ended there.

Roni's Early Loss Story

"My mom had been in and out of the hospital for some time," Roni said, "but I wasn't prepared for her to die when she did. Even though my mother had been inoculated with the Salk vaccine, she contracted polio. Ultimately, she experienced respiratory failure and died in an iron lung when she was pregnant with her third child. The baby, who was due on March seventeenth, died with my mom on December fifth."

I felt shock and extreme sadness as Roni shared this story. Losing an unborn sibling and a mother at the same time felt doubly tragic. Then, Roni back-tracked to the last time she saw her mother alive and what that experience meant to her as she shared her own "last words" story.

"As I was leaving the room on the last night I visited her, my mother called after me saying, 'Roni, don't ever forget that I love you.' Because of these beautiful last words, I never felt angry at her for dying. Instead, I was strengthened, knowing that I had something to hold on to for the rest of my life."

As we exchanged stories, Roni also reflected on her father experience as she was growing up.

"My father was low on praise. No matter how well I did he said, 'You did what was expected.' I often felt like he didn't care about me. My brother was younger and I thought he got all of the attention. I kept thinking that no one was helping me."

Roni experienced pain due to feelings of isolation and a lack of love. She gave me an example. "Once, when my grandmother told me to go get dressed, she later found me crying in my bedroom. The tears came because I was thinking, *If I had a mother, she would have told me what to wear.* I don't remember my grandmother responding to my tears. She was an impatient person and dealing with her own grief—the loss of her daughter and then my grandfather just three months later. Those were difficult years for me and my family."

When I asked Roni what advice she would give other motherless daughters, she shared two quotes. One was her own: "What you do with your life is your choice." The other was from author Anthony DeMello who she quoted as writing, "No one can hurt you; no one can make you sad. You have a choice." Roni added, "I pass these quotes along, as they have helped me journey to a place of peace and fulfillment." Roni acknowledged her early pain but also delighted in the opportunity to recall her past and celebrate how far she had come.

Although Vicki had a very different mother loss story to tell, like Roni and I, she too had a special "last words experience" she wanted to share.

Vicki and I met in the early '70s. As stay-at-home mothers of young children, we became good friends through a weekly women's Bible study group. Although we both eventually moved away from the area, we renewed our friendship through Facebook. This recent connection was how I discovered that Vicki's mother, Myra Scovel, died in 1994 as a result of Alzheimer's disease.

I was particularly interested in Myra's later story because, as long-ago friends, Vicki shared fascinating tales about her parents and her own early life in Asia. For instance, because her parents were missionaries and the family was living in an area without adequate English-speaking schools, Vicki was sent to Woodstock, a boarding school in northern India.

Coincidently, this was the same school where my daughter, Winnie, worked decades later.

Vicki began her story by celebrating who her mother was before Alzheimer's disease claimed her.

Vicki's Alzheimer's Loss Story

"My parents were medical missionaries in China for twenty-one years and in India for six. My father, Frederick Scovel, was a medical doctor. My mother was an author. In 1943, when my mother was pregnant with me, my parents were held in a concentration camp in north China for six months following the Japanese invasion of China. During their imprisonment, my dad gathered eggshells for my mom from the officers' garbage, which she then ground up and drank in hot water to provide calcium for me as a growing fetus.

"Later that year, my parents were released from the camp and boarded a Swedish ship, the *Gripsholm*, to bring them back to the United States. I was born, three weeks late, on the day the ship docked in New York City. The story of my birth made the front pages of the New York newspapers. We returned to China when I was two and we were there when the Communist regime took over. Our family ended up under house arrest for several months before being released in 1951."

Although I never met her in person, I always thought of Vicki's mother as a brave adventurer and respected author of books like *The Ginger Jars* which told of the dangerous days she experienced in China. It was especially difficult to imagine her suffering from Alzheimer's disease. Vicki sounded sad as she recalled her mother's early life and how it contrasted to her life after the disease set in. "To watch my mother regress was the opposite of watching a baby grow. It was like the same process in reverse.

"When my mother started showing symptoms of Alzheimer's shortly before turning eighty, she told my five siblings and me that she would prefer to live in a nursing home rather than with one of us and be a burden. It made our decision easier when we had to do exactly that.

"My mother always said she would die at the age of eighty-nine and, sure enough, ten days after her eighty-ninth birthday she passed away in a fetal position. She returned just as she arrived."

After Vicki reminisced a bit more about her mother's life, she said, "I must tell you this one last story about my mother. My mom was very passive and hadn't spoken for about two years. However, one day while I was visiting her—just sitting with her really—she turned, looked straight at me and said, 'I love you, Vicki.' I was stunned for a moment, and then I realized she had given me a precious good-bye gift."

At the close of our conversation, I asked Vicki if she was worried about the heredity factor of the disease that claimed her mother.

"Of course," she said, "there is concern about passing on the Alzheimer's gene, but we try to keep a sense of humor about it. For instance, when my grown son asked me if I thought I'd get Alzheimer's like his grandmother, I replied, 'No, David' . . . his name is Mike."

Vicki treasures her mom-memories from the past and prefers to remember her mother as the creative adventurer she was prior to Alzheimer's claiming her.

Talking with daughters like Vicki and Roni and writing about the last weeks of my mother's life helped me bring old and new feelings to the surface and think of my mother as a real person—not just an abstract, distant memory. Remembering my loss and sharing stories with other daughters gave me greater empathy for those who have had life changing experiences. I'm good with a quick cry and moving on. Now I'm better equipped to understand the profound impact of mother loss and how it's a life changing event whether we are tuned into it or not. Telling my story, even after so many years, made a difference. I hope you too will gain insight and understanding of yourself and others as you tell or retell your story.

Jerome Bruner, psychologist, once said, "The eagerness to tell one's story signals a desire to live." As we tell our mother loss stories we affirm not only our desire to live, but to thrive. We share so others can benefit from our experience and we learn about ourselves in the telling.

Now What?

Take time to recall your mother loss story. Remember your feelings—happy, sad, mad— whatever emotions come up for you. Be still. Breathe deeply. Take a moment to look deep inside, reflect on and accept where you've been and where you are today. Listen to your heart and your intuition as you get in touch with your memories and feelings. Now, share your mother loss story with a person you trust.

Coaching Questions

- If you've never shared your full story or haven't shared it in many years, with whom might you confide?

- What difference do you think sharing your story will make in your life and in the life of the person with whom you're sharing?

- If you had a "last words experience," reflect on how it impacted your life. What is one outcome you had from your mother's last words?

REACH OUT FOR HELP

Be strong, be fearless, be beautiful.
Believe that anything is possible when you
have the right people there to support you.

—Misty Copeland, American ballet dancer

Whether we reach out to a family member, mental health professional, mother loss support group, grief group, clergy, or online platform, we can benefit from the support of others when we are facing the loss of a loved one. Women particularly find comfort through talk therapy or other opportunities to process their emotions.

Early Loss Help

According to Hope Edelman, author of *Motherless Daughters: The Legacy of Loss,* and other experts in the mother loss field, it's important to remember that a daughter can only process grief at her current cognitive ability. For instance, an early loss daughter may feel some resolution until she experiences a big life event like marriage, divorce, motherhood or any time in her life when she "knows" more about her loss. Realizing how young and vulnerable she was or how important her mother's input would have been to her decisions, she stumbles into sadness and, once again, may need support as she experiences the long arc of grief. In my experience, divorce triggered the need to seek therapy. At the time, I had no idea that my early loss experience played a role but I learned that it's never too late to reach out for help.

Since 1969, when Kübler-Ross' book, *On Death and Dying*, proposed the five stages of grief, many professionals have pointed to these stages as they worked with daughters in their "recovery." In 1996, however, authors Klass, Silverman, and Nickman shed light on an important new bereavement concept—the "continuing bonds theory." Their work questioned linear models of grief like Ross's that were supposed to lead to things like acceptance, detachment, and new life. Dennis Klass, in his book *Continuing Bonds: New Understandings of Grief,* makes the observation that when a loved one dies you slowly find ways to adjust and redefine your relationship with that person. This allows for a continued bond that will endure, in different ways and to varying degrees, throughout your life. When I read about this concept I realized that it was only in writing this book that I established a "continuing bond" with my mother.

Like me, Gray is also an early loss daughter who sought therapy years after her mother died. I met Gray in an online motherless daughters' support group. She said that it was difficult for her to talk about her mother and it would be more comfortable for her to answer questions via email. Gray's mother died at age thirty-six on Gray's tenth birthday. "Not a great memory," she wrote.

Gray's Early Loss Story

> After my mother died, I was bumped around. When my dad remarried, he and my stepmom took care of me. The relationship I had with my stepmother was incredibly dysfunctional and emotionally draining. Because of this rocky relationship, I was sent to my mom's brother and his wife when I was sixteen. My aunt and I had a great relationship but we didn't have a real mom-like connection.

Because Gray was only twenty-five when she contacted me, experiences with her stepmother and aunt were still fresh in her mind. Gray continues.

> Seeing other people with their mothers is always hard. I was recently present when my boyfriend's first niece was born. Seeing his mother with his sister really knocked me out emotionally knowing I will never have that kind of an experience. My mom died due to drug addiction and I've not really forgiven her. My brother has been more outwardly emotional about her death and has more difficulty talking about it than I do. The experience has brought us closer.

According to an article in the *Journal of American Psychiatry*, a child whose mother died by suicide or an accident such as drug overdose or drug addiction is at higher risk for depression than a child whose mother died from a natural illness. Also, if the daughter suffered from depression prior to the mother's death or she felt accountable for the parent's death, she is also more likely to experience depression within two years of the loss when compared to her peers. In her email, Gray confided that she continues to suffer from depression.

> I don't know if it's directly related to my mother's death but I'm sure it's part of it. I had to grow up fast so I definitely think her death made me more resilient and determined to be independent. I think the best thing I ever did for myself was to get into therapy. There I was able to finally go through my emotions and discuss the impact my mother's death had on me.

Help For A Young Family Member

Through my interviews and research, I've learned that every child's mother loss experience is different and not all children or adults suffer from depression as a result. However, if you are an adult reading this book to gain insight in order to help a younger child who has experienced mother loss, it's important to recognize depression in order to seek professional help if warranted.

Here are some signs to look for. Children who are depressed may feel misunderstood, guilty, hopeless, or angry. They may withdraw from their family and friends, and show changes in their sleeping and eating habits. School performance may decline or they may avoid school and social activities by having physical complaints like stomachache or headache.

Daughters who lose their mothers as young adults can also benefit from therapy or other professional help. This age of mother loss is often overlooked as a demographic. As daughters in their early 20's test out their identities, mother loss can be particularly destabilizing.

Kate Andres who was referred to me by a mutual friend, lost her mother to colon cancer when Andres was twenty-four. Andres emailed me much of her mother loss story prior to our speaking on the phone.

Kate's Young Adult Loss Story

In the last few days of her life, my mother, Deborah Harris Seymour, was at a beautiful hospice center in Branford, Connecticut with ocean view rooms. I visited her every day, sharing many special moments. I had decided to get my Masters in Social Work in Connecticut so I could be close to her that last year. She told me to always keep my heart open and that I would be a wonderful mother someday.

On the last day of her life, I was alone with her as she struggled to breathe. Although I was scared and didn't want her to go, the hospice nurses instructed me to tell her it was okay and that I loved her. I repeated the words that I wished I didn't have to say. For many years these dying moments haunted me and led to nightmares. There are physical things that occur in the body when someone dies and witnessing these was difficult for me to sit with. I think that was the traumatic piece.

As Andres experienced, saying good-bye to a dying person isn't easy. Yet, if possible, it's important for a mother and her daughter to do so. According to hospice professionals and the National Institute on Aging, it's vital to take advantage of opportunities when the person is awake and communicative to facilitate the "saying good-bye" process. If the dying person isn't lucid, or is in a coma, remember that hearing is the last sense to leave. Assume everything you say can be heard and understood, even if the person is not responsive. Never speak about the dying person as if she is not in the room.

Even with all the preparation and knowledge that death is coming, the moment of death is not easy to see. Even those who are closest to the dying person may choose to be absent. The decision to be with a loved one depends on many things.

Although Andres's mother died in her presence, hospice experts say it's not uncommon for a dying person to wait to die after loved ones have left the room. If you suspect this may be true, based on your mother's personality or her circumstances, make sure you allow for this. Sometimes, if a person seems to be holding on, you may simply say, "I'm going to leave the room for awhile. I love you."

Sometimes the help you need is factual. Knowing what active dying might look like may help a daughter feel less fearful. Here are the signs and symptoms of dying from the Crossroads Hospice and Palliative Care website:

- Long pauses in breathing; patient's breathing patterns may also be very irregular

- Patient is in a coma, or semi-coma, or cannot be awoken

- Urinary and bowel incontinence and/or decrease in urine; urine may also be discolored

- Blood pressure drops significantly

- Patient's skin changes color (mottling) and their extremities may feel cold to the touch

- Hallucinations, delirium, and agitation

- Build-up of fluid in the lungs, which may cause unusual gurgling sounds

Prior to the active dying stage, experts recommend you say three things to a dying person, for their sake as well as yours: "You will not be alone (if this is appropriate); you will feel no pain (if it's true); we will be okay."

Andres continued sharing her mother loss story beginning with what happened after her mother's death and how she found help.

> About a year after my mother died, I went to a day-long grief seminar, which was helpful in my recovery. Also, my best friend from a motherless daughters' support group I attended was a sounding board for me. Her mother hung herself in their basement when my friend was in college. We talked about the raw stuff of death. You can't talk about the ending details with just anyone. Being able to talk about them with a friend who understood was helpful.
>
> Although my experience of my mother's last moments felt traumatic to me for many years, now I find so much beauty in it. She brought me into the world and I had the honor of being with her when she left. In addition to talking with my friend, I found healing through therapy and simply the passage of time.

Death By Suicide Information

When I read about Andres's friend whose mother died by suicide I did some research. I learned that when a mother dies in this way, the effect is even more painful and potentially disturbing than from other types of death.

Researchers at Johns Hopkins Children's Center found that children who are under eighteen when their parent commits suicide are three times as likely as children with living parents to later commit suicide themselves. Lead investigator, Holly C. Wilcox, Ph.D., a psychiatric epidemiologist writes, "However, it's likely that developmental, environmental and genetic factors all come together, most likely simultaneously, to increase risk."

As I read further, I discovered that the likelihood of a daughter's suicide increases when the parent who commits suicide is the mother. In these circumstances, it is critical to treat the daughter for the trauma of sudden loss and break the cycle of suicide.

It's Never Too Late to Get Help - My Story

Like many daughters, I too found working with a therapist to be extremely beneficial. I sought out Barbra McCoy Getz, Licensed Clinical Social Worker (LCSW), for therapy in 1989 and worked with her individually for a year. Prior to working with Barbra, I worked briefly with two other therapists who initially identified my need to address mother loss issues. Although I sought therapy to help me through a divorce, I realized, thirty-five years after my mother's death, how early mother loss had impacted my life.

Barbra helped me get in touch with my issues around abandonment, intimacy, and my inability to express a wide range of emotions. I also learned I was judgmental and could come across as one who feels superior even when that was not my intention. Later, my husband and I went to Barbra for marital counseling. After we made the decision to divorce, I continued with Barbra and became part of a therapy group consisting of six women.

During the years I participated in this weekly group therapy, I learned many things about myself including how to be less judgmental of others. Being entrusted with the deepest secrets of five women with very diverse personal issues, I had the opportunity to practice active listening, empathy, and caring about women from a variety of backgrounds.

Barbra was a positive role model for acceptance and setting boundaries. In addition, we had creative assignments like acting out our life story without words, experiencing interpretive dance, and creating handmade gifts depicting how we felt about one another. As you'll learn in Step Four, these activities taught us how tapping into our creativity can help us get in touch with our emotions and physical bodies.

I found the interpretive dance the most daunting of our creative exercises. Using my body to express my emotions was foreign to me. Just getting in touch with my emotions was a challenge. However, as I went from holding my arms close to my body and moving in a small circle to flying, unselfconsciously, across the room, I gained a greater understanding of the many ways emotions can be felt and expressed.

The scariest part of group therapy for me was an anger exercise in which we were all expected to participate. I had never "seen" anger. This may seem strange but my dad was the type of personality who rarely, if ever, raised his voice. If he was angry with me, he spoke quietly with a serious tone of voice. This was very impactful. My husband and I didn't exhibit outright anger towards each other and I used my dad's parenting approach with my children.

During our anger exercise, the shouting, punching of pillows, and other outward manifestations of anger were very foreign and frightening to me. In fact, the fear of seeing anger exhibited in such a way was so frightening it caused me to bolt from the room. Barbra brought me back. She recognized that learning how to express a wide range of emotions, including sadness and anger, was one of the reasons I was in therapy and one of the life lessons I needed to learn to be a more fully functioning adult. Looking back, I understand how fortunate I was to see anger manifested in a safe environment. Although anger still frightens me to some extent, thanks to therapy, I've come a long way in my ability to express and accept a full range of emotions in myself and others.

In 1993, Barbra referred me to a Motherless Daughters' Support Group led by Gale Vance, LCSW. I participated in two, eight-week motherless daughters groups led by Gale. Through the groups, I was affirmed in my progress and process. Primarily, I recognized, more than ever, how my dad's devotion to me and his faithful parenting made a significant difference in my life.

Years later, Gale was also instrumental in helping me contact many of the early loss daughters I interviewed for this book. A motherless daughter herself, Gale has a personal understanding coupled with professional expertise.

Gale became involved with motherless daughters after she and her sister were visiting a library in New York City in the mid-1990's and inadvertently met Hope Edelman, author of the best-selling book, *Motherless Daughters: The Legacy of Loss*, who was speaking about her book at an author's event there.

It was at this event that Gale learned about Edelman's groundbreaking book and motherless daughters' support groups.

When asked about these early groups, Edelman responded by email.

Oh my gosh, Gale Vance! Yes, I remember that she was an early group leader. This was back in the mid-1990s when there was a Motherless Daughters, Inc. 501c3 nonprofit based in New York City. I'd started it with a small group of women soon after the book came out. When I moved to California in 1997 they kept it going for a while but it shut down a few years later. The Internet existed by then and women were able to find each other online and wanted to make local connections, so they were able to do it that way faster and easier.

In the 1990s the nonprofit oversaw about 30 support groups around the US and Canada. Gale is correct, we wanted leaders to either be therapists or have extensive prior training to lead support groups, since sensitive material often came up in the circles. We had a format that shared with group leaders and asked them to follow in exchange for use of the Motherless Daughters Support Group name, which was trademarked. After the non-profit shut down, the trademark lapsed, and the groups you see today around the world now all operate independently. I have a best-practices document I share with anyone who's interested in starting a group, but after that I serve only as an informal resource and listing site (www.hopeedelman.com/support-groups). Each group sets its own guidelines and meets how and when they choose. That's the best way to find a local group right now.

Also, as an additional detail, the loose network is called Motherless Daughters Support Groups since a number of them are peer-led social groups now and are often free of charge. Therapy groups would be led by a licensed counselor and most likely charge a fee.

As a long-time group leader, I asked Gale to share her observations regarding motherless daughters. We spoke on the phone.

"Of course, there is a whole range of reactions to mother loss. The critical factor, in my experience, is not so much the death of the mother but what happened to the daughter after her death. Did the father emotionally disappear, become an alcoholic, quickly remarry? Was the mother's death never spoken of, was there no reminiscing about the mother, was the daughter shuffled off to grandparents or other relatives?

"Some daughters never deal with their feelings. They are stuffed down and the fact of their mother's death becomes a secret. Daughters often have abandonment issues and never want to become emotionally attached again. This is the result of living from their fears. However, as daughters who have experienced early mother loss express themselves and relate with other women with similar stories, they often begin to heal and are affirmed in their process."

We then moved our conversation from Gale's therapy clients and her knowledge of the subject of mother loss to her personal experience. Gale was seventeen when her mother died at the age of forty.

Gale's Teenage Loss Story

"After I read Hope's mother loss book, I felt affirmed in the fact that I handled my mother's death in a fairly healthy way. After her death, I became involved in many after-school activities, which I later learned is not unusual."

Gale continued, "My mother was sick for three years prior to her death. My brothers were only four-and-a-half and seven-and-a-half. My sister was twelve. My brothers have few, if any, memories of our mother. Our grandmother came to live with us after my mother died.

"Fortunately, I had a great dad. In later years, my brothers told me they felt abandoned when I left home as a young adult. I had no idea I was so important to them."

Gale's statement about her brothers reminded me of my dad. He seemed content to be single for the ten years after my mother died—until I went away to college. Even over the phone I could tell he was depressed. Within eighteen months of my leaving, my dad remarried. Like Gale, I was surprised to learn how much my presence contributed to my dad's happiness and well-being.

Although living in different states, Gale and her siblings remain close and get together at least once a year. "We suffered a unique loss and learned that family is important. We are still a support system for each other."

Gale was divorced in her early thirties and never remarried. "It was important for me to find out if I could make it on my own. I was frightened of the possibility, but I proved my fears were groundless."

In addition to learning she could live independently, Gale also feels that as a result of her mother's death, she matured early and was a deeper thinker at a younger age. In fact, Gale's first career was in medical research, which she felt demonstrated how she addressed her early emotional needs. "I wanted to feel empowered," Gale said.

Now in her late seventies, Gale has confronted her fears, embraced her family, and found a way to flourish in the years after her mother's death. In her role as therapist, Gale made a significant difference in the lives of other women, helping them realize they were not alone as they forged a path forward after mother loss.

Seeking Help When Dealing with Dementia/Alzheimer's

Having a mother with dementia can be challenging both before and after the parent dies. Daughters and other family members can benefit from professional help and the opportunity to gain knowledge of the disease.

As past Board Chair of Friendship Senior Options, a dual-campus senior living organization in the Chicagoland area, I knew Kate Aylward, Life Services Coordinator and Memory Support Case Manager for Friendship Village. Aylward's role as a case manager is to undertake assessment, monitoring, planning, advocacy and linking of the patient and her family with information and support services. I called and asked Kate to address the availability of and need for professional help for daughters who had mothers diagnosed with dementia or Alzheimer's disease.

"Every experience of a daughter losing her mother to Alzheimer's, or other forms of dementia, is unique," Kate said. "Each person handles it in a different way. Seeking help from case managers, support groups, and other sources is very important in helping the daughter realize that her mother's behavior is no one's fault."

I understood what Kate was saying. I knew from my experience in long term care that blame is a common response when there is a lack of knowledge about the progression and effects of Alzheimer's and other forms of dementia. Family members may blame the person with the disease for her lack of self-care which they perceive caused the disease or blame caregivers who they see as being unable to contain the symptoms. "Yes," agreed Kate. "People frequently come to negative and inaccurate conclusions when they are frightened and don't understand the facts of the disease.

"Daughters may also find it difficult to accept their mothers when they develop new relationships and interests. People with dementia often bond with people outside their previous sphere." In my experience, it's not unusual for a personal relationship to form between a man and woman even though their partners are alive. This can be very disconcerting to a daughter if, for instance, she sees her mother holding hands with a strange man because she no longer remembers her husband.

Kate continued, "If a daughter doesn't have a good understanding of the nature of dementia, she may take it personally when her mother no longer recognizes her or other family members."

Aylward went on to describe other scenarios in which a case manager can be helpful. "Some family members joke about the possibility of having dementia in the future. It seems that humor often masks their fears. Their own future may become an impetus for gaining a greater understanding of the disease. As a case manager within a longterm care facility, I work with families every step of the way to help them understand the disease, their reactions to what is happening to their mother, and what the future will look like. Daughters need to take advantage of this resource. Referrals can be made if family members need therapy or more extensive help beyond what is offered by a case manager."

To get a glimpse into the daughter's side of the story, Aylward connected me with "Amy."

Amy was willing to speak with me on the phone about her mother but didn't want to share identifying information.

Amy's Alzheimer's Loss Story

"My ninety-year-old mother is not yet lost to me. She still recognizes me, my husband, and after a bit, my siblings. They live out of state and she doesn't see them as frequently, so it takes her longer to recall their faces. With other family and friends, my mom frequently pretends to recognize them, but I can tell from the look on her face that she has no idea who they are.

"My mom is at the blessed stage where she has forgotten she has memory loss. Her life now is much less frustrating for her than it was eight years ago when she was first diagnosed with Alzheimer's."

I spoke with other women whose mothers suffered from dementia and learned that this "blessed stage," as Amy calls it, is the moment daughters both yearn for and dread. The period when a mother is no longer frustrated with, nor fears, the disease, feels like a silver lining or a gift. And yet, it also means the disease is progressing toward a time when she will no longer recognize her daughter. I was delighted to hear that Amy was staying in the present as she spent time with her mother.

Living in an assisted care memory unit enables Amy's mother a certain amount of independence even though she has virtually no short-term memory. Amy explains, "If I leave the room and return in a few minutes, to my mother it's as if I have just arrived." This experience is just another stop along the long road Amy has shared with her mom and dementia.

"When my mom and dad lived out of state and we only saw them a few times a year, we thought all was well. When they decided to move to Illinois to be closer to us and we saw them regularly, that's when my husband and I recognized the symptoms of dementia. It was more difficult for her to mask her state of mind and we finally realized how far my mom had declined and how difficult caring for her had been for my dad."

In spite of her mother's illness, Amy is finding joy being with her mom. "She lights up when I come into the room. I lived out of state my whole adult life. Now, at sixty-three, I have this special time with my mother, which I didn't have before. Even though we have switched roles and I am now the parent, it's still a bonding experience for us. I have renewed love and passion for her because it feels like I'm dealing with my child."

Although Amy has wonderful support from her husband, daughters, and extended family, she recommends attending a caregiver class. Amy wishes she had attended earlier to have received the extra support she needed when she first recognized her mother's decline. Taking the class later, however, helped Amy realize she wasn't the only daughter on this journey.

"I also recommend finding a good geriatrician for your parent. Specializing in the elderly, these doctors have a very different point of view than that of a regular family physician and they can be extremely helpful." Amy also encouraged caregivers to seek individual therapy if they need it. "It has done wonders for me."

Amy concluded our phone conversation with a lovely story.

"As a human resources professional, I gave the following advice to my colleagues who had to answer annoying, recurring questions from their clients, 'Answer like it's the first time you've heard it.' Now this advice is helping me communicate with my mother. I don't say, 'Mother, you just told me that, or asked me that, or remembered that.' Instead, I make every effort to treat her repetitions like they are the first time I've heard them. After all, to her they are the first."

Amy educated herself about the progression of Alzheimer's so she will know what she and her mother face in the future and to be better prepared for the ups and downs of caregiving.

Like Amy, Jean's mother also had Alzheimer's and found a support group beneficial. In fact, I met Jean through her support group on Facebook and she agreed to share her story.

Jean's Alzheimer's Loss Story

"My mother was diagnosed with Alzheimer's in 2010. Four years later, she died at the age of seventy-six. My stepfather, who was ten years older than my mother, developed vascular dementia and died five days after his wife.

"I had two siblings. One died when he was twenty-three. The other died after my mother was diagnosed. Mother asked about my sister all the time, but I never told her that she had passed away. Because of the dementia, she was spared the suffering of losing another child.

"Initially my parents went through the process while living together. Later, because my stepdad developed physical problems, he had to be moved to a skilled care facility at another location. When they still knew one another, I made arrangements for them to see each other occasionally. It was very difficult when they parted.

"My advice to daughters is to expect your mother to change completely. You'll be dealing with a new person."

Amy found that reaching out for help early on was beneficial to deal with this change in her mother and advised others to do the same.

"Get to grief counseling as soon as your mother is diagnosed. This will help you when situations like the following arise. At the end, my mother would say 'I love you' right out of the blue. Then, the next day, she would call me 'rotten bitch.' The week before she went into a coma she said, 'Thank you for everything.' I should have known that the end was near."

In addition to seeking early grief counseling, Jean also started her own Facebook page and is involved with several support groups.

With content taken from journals she wrote when her parents were sick, Jean wrote the book, *This Daughter Still Cries*, to help others through this difficult life event. The combination of seeking help early and writing about her experiences enabled Jean to begin to move forward after her dual loss.

Carrie, another daughter who lost her mother to dementia, sought help from professional sources but also from one that surprised her. Carrie connected with me from information she found on my mother loss blog. Although she felt it would be extremely difficult for her to talk about her mother because she had died just six months prior to our call, Carrie said she wanted to share her story in order to help other daughters feel less alone in their grief.

Carrie's Alzheimer's Loss Story

"After my mother retired, she very gradually began to show symptoms of dementia," Carrie began. "She lost a lot of weight and explained it to me by saying she just got so busy she forgot to eat. She was diagnosed with Alzheimer's about three years before her death."

Carrie, a forty-three-year-old teacher of the Deaf, lived with her mother in order to save money as she worked in the high-priced San Francisco Bay Area. "My parents divorced when I was three and I'm an only child. My mom and I were always very close. We were a team. I'm single and my mom was my very best friend. Living together bonded us further."

By the time Carrie and her mother mutually decided to visit a doctor for an evaluation, her mother couldn't complete the test that required her to draw a clock, yet she was still driving. Six or seven months later, her mother fell in the night and broke her hip. "I think the trauma of the fall accelerated my mother's Alzheimer's disease. Before her accident, she was still independent. After the accident, I had to hire a full-time caregiver for the hours I was at work. Later, we had to have two caregivers when I was away because she could no longer walk or stand by herself. In the end, just three years after her diagnosis, my mother contracted pneumonia, could no longer swallow, and died. She was seventy-four and, prior to the disease, in very good health, always exercising and eating right."

As the interview progressed, Carrie became tearful as she shared a meaningful, "last words" memory from shortly before her mother died. "My mom talked a lot, but what she said made no sense, it was mostly just gibberish. Then one day I said to her, 'We're best friends' to which my mom replied, 'We certainly are.' It was a moment I will always cherish."

I felt Carrie's grief and love for her mother when she told me that she still cries every day. "I took care of my mom twenty-four hours a day, seven days a week when I wasn't working and now I just don't know what to do with myself. I'm glad I was able to keep her at home with the help of hospice."

Carrie is doing what she can to move forward in a healthy way by going to a parental loss support group and accepting the grief counseling hospice offered her. She suggested that daughters who are in the midst of caring for their mothers find out everything they can about the disease so they can be their mother's advocate.

"Sometimes you have to fight for yourself and for your mother. Arm yourself with knowledge!" Not only did Carrie educate herself about her mother's disease, she educated others. "Even my middle school students have learned about Alzheimer's through me. When my mom died, they made me a big card. It is very special to me.

"Another piece of advice is to research home health organizations who supply caregivers and find out which ones are the most reliable. Your hospice contact can help you with this."

Tearfully ending our interview, Carrie said, "I still have thirty or so years to live without my best friend. It is hard to bear." My heart went out to Carrie as I wished her well in her journey.

When a daughter loses her mother due to homicide, it is especially important for her to seek help from a professional. If you have recently experienced mother loss, Katie's experience may be too graphic to read at this time. If this is true for you, please skip ahead and come back to this story when you feel ready.

I met Kate in a mother loss support group on Facebook. We spoke on the phone six months after her mother loss experience. "When you asked if we could talk, I knew it would be difficult," said Kate. "I'm on the phone with you today because I want my story to make a difference in the lives of other daughters who have had a similar traumatic event in their lives. In the past couple of months, I have sought information from daughters who have experienced loss in a similar way and found very little. Thanks for the opportunity to tell about the circumstances that led up to my mother's murder by my stepfather on January 29, 2018."

Katie's Homicide Loss Story

Katie became concerned when her mother didn't call to check in about her grandson's recent medical procedure. She called her mother and, when she didn't answer, Katie called her stepfather. He said she was sick, had taken pain pills, and was sleeping.

"I just knew she was dead, but my sister thought I was being ridiculous and wanted to wait to intervene. Since she was the one who lived in the same town as my mother and would be the one to make the personal contact, we waited. However, after three days of no communication from our mom, my sister also became alarmed and called me at two in the morning on January 31st. While I was on the phone with her, my sister drove the short distance to our mother's house.

"I suddenly heard gunshots. Our stepfather had coaxed my sister inside the house then shot her twice in the face. She played dead and I immediately called 911. This all happened in Oklahoma, I was in Texas.

"When the police arrived, they were met at the door by my stepfather holding a gun. They shot him dead. My stepfather's brother was in the house, enlisted, no doubt, to help clean up after killing my mother and was arrested for failure to stop a killing. My mother's body was found in the back of her car, which was parked in their driveway. My stepfather was about to leave with her in the trunk when my sister arrived."

As I listened to Katie's dramatic story, I felt overwhelmed by the violence, grief, and trauma these sisters endured. With only a slight hesitancy in her voice, Katie pushed on to relate the background of her story.

"The seeds of this tragic experience were planted years earlier. My mother divorced our birth father when we were very young. We moved in with our grandparents until my mother remarried when I was about ten or eleven. No one liked my stepfather. He was verbally abusive from the start.

When I was thirteen we moved to Oklahoma. I had always been close to my mom but our relationship began to change. She wasn't the same. My stepfather created a wedge between us and she was always trying to sell him to us. I didn't feel like I could tell her anything because she would relay it to him and there would be trouble."

At the time, Katie wasn't sure her mother was being physically abused but her intuition told her something was wrong. In fact, Katie and her sister began to notice bruises on their mother and questioned her about them.

"My mom explained her bruises by telling us she had fallen or had some other kind of accident. We did find out later, after her murder, that she told a co-worker that if anything happened to her it would be because of Bill, her husband. When we heard this we knew she had been frightened for a long time.

"My grandma, husband, friends, and co-workers have been great. It's weird because sometimes I need people around me and other times I just want to be alone. My therapist's mom is also dead, so I feel like she understands me. My sister made a full physical recovery after being shot. However, like me, she is also in therapy to help her deal with the issues surrounding this experience."

I felt relief to know that Katie was seeing a therapist. According to the National Center for Victims of Crime (NCVC), there are many ways to feel when someone close to you is murdered. You may feel overcome with disbelief, anger, and sadness with an intensity never experienced before, or you may feel emotionally numb. It is normal for adults and children to experience intense feelings in the months, and years, following a homicide. According to

NCVC, survivors are at risk of developing post-traumatic stress disorder (PTSD) and other problems, where extreme anxiety, fear, sadness or nightmares and intrusive thoughts remain constant for weeks or months. As Katie has learned, support and counseling are often very helpful in managing these overwhelming emotions.

"At first I was angry with my mom rather than being angry with my stepfather. I kept thinking to myself, *Why did she bring this man into our lives?* I'm no longer mad at her but it took a while. Although my therapist has helped me move forward, I still feel very isolated as a daughter who lost her mother to murder."

When I asked her what advice she wanted to give daughters in similar situations, she said, "Go to a grief therapist, preferably one who has had a similar experience, and don't be afraid to take medication if you need it for anxiety or whatever. It's okay to be angry, sad, confused. Take care of yourself. Right now I feel like it's acceptable if my kids eat McDonalds more than they normally would. Finally, don't be afraid to tell people when you need to be alone."

As difficult as it was for Katie to share her story so soon after her mother's murder, I felt honored to be the recipient of her account of what happened. Katie was grateful for the opportunity to share with other daughters since information about situations like hers is so scarce.

In her book, *Trauma and Recover: The Aftermath of Violence,* Judith Lewis Herman addresses experiences such as Katie's.

The ordinary response to atrocities is to banish them from consciousness. Certain violations of the social contract are too terrible to utter aloud: this is the meaning of the word unspeakable. Atrocities, however, refuse to be buried. Equally as powerful as the desire to deny atrocities is the conviction that denial does not work. Folk wisdom is filled with ghosts who refuse to rest in their graves until their stories are told. Murder will out. Remembering and telling the truth about terrible events are prerequisites both for the restoration of the social order and for the healing of individual victims.

Katie's story is a dramatic example of the importance of reaching out for help to examine the truth, tell our stories, and begin our healing process. I'm a believer in the value of therapy and support groups to assist daughters as they move forward. Who among us doesn't need help understanding our feelings, our past, our relationships, and what might be ahead as our loved ones age. Whether you seek therapy, counseling, or other professional help during your mother's illness, soon after your loss, or years later, the experience is likely to help you get in touch with repressed feelings, serve as a sounding board for life decisions, and validate your process and progress.

Now What?

If you have not experienced therapy, counseling, coaching or other professional help since your mother loss, consider what value it might bring you. This second step in the process of moving forward can be taken at any time in your life. It's never too late.

Coaching Questions

- In regards to the death of your mother, what emotional baggage, if any, do you carry? What would it be like to have someone help you lighten your load?

- If you've felt the need to reach out for help but have resisted, consider what's holding you back. Is it not knowing where to turn, embarrassment, finances, wanting to keep your emotions bottled up for fear of what they might reveal? What will help you to override your resistance?

- To whom might you turn to begin this process? Your family doctor, clergy, community mental health organization, the Internet—all might be resources to help you get started. Some community mental health centers provide therapy on a sliding income scale. Check it out if finances are an issue.

STEP THREE

ANTICIPATE THE ANNIVERSARY YEAR(S)

*It happened in New York, April 10th, nineteen years
ago. Even my hand balks at the date. I had to push
to write it down, just to keep the pen moving on
the paper. It used to be a perfectly ordinary day, but
now it sticks up on the calendar like a rusty nail.*

—Donna Tartt, author of *The Goldfinch*

There is a year nearly every daughter who has lost her mother describes as being "very significant." This is the year when she becomes the age of her mother when she died. This was also true for me.

My Anniversary Story

When I turned thirty-four, the age my mother was when she died, I had a serious uterine infection. The doctor prescribed antibiotics but my infection wasn't responding. Finally, my fever was so high and I was in so much pain, the doctor sent me to the hospital. I was bent in half as I sat in the wheelchair for the nurse to take me to my room. They put me on an intravenous antibiotic, daily penicillin shots, and ordered an ultrasound. The test showed a mass in the area. The doctor was baffled about its origins but, in my mind, the elephant in the room was named Uterine Cancer. The doctor decided to repeat the ultrasound the next day after the antibiotics had a chance to kick in.

The circumstances felt ominous to me. I feared that I was about to be the third generation of women to die at an early age. Unlike most early loss daughters—until this moment—I hadn't given much thought to the anniversary of my mother's death, nor her mother's. But, on this long and anxious day, I did the math. I realized I was the age my mother was when she died. Further, my oldest daughter was the same age I had been. Had the unconscious knowledge of the anniversary of my mother's death been so impactful that it triggered this health crisis? Now that I recognized how the dates coincided, would this recognition impede my recovery? There were many unanswered questions.

In the evening, my little girls, ages eight and three, came with their dad to visit me. We named the intravenous stand "Fred" so it would seem less scary to them. We walked the hall so they could see me out of bed. Was I remembering the days I'd spent visiting my mom in the hospital? I believe my intuition was telling me to consider my daughters' possible fearful feelings more than the average hospitalized mom might. I knew what it was like to have a mother never return from the hospital. I also had experienced losing a mother at a young age and I didn't want them to imagine they too could be motherless.

When I was eight and my mother was ill, I turned to God for solace and intervention. Now sick myself, I again turned to God in prayer. I knew I needed to be clear and ask for what I wanted. Here's what I said:

"Dear God, as you know, Winnie, is the same age I was when my mother died. She is independent, strong, and has a great dad. She will be fine. But, I have this little girl, Katie. She is only three years old, much too young to be left without a mother. Sorry God, I can't leave her yet. I'm not going now. Please stand with me on this. Amen."

The next day my husband came to the hospital by himself to be with me as we heard the results of the second ultrasound. Dr. Johnson looked bewildered as he entered my hospital room late in the afternoon.

"The mass is completely gone," he said. He had no explanation as to the cause of the mass or the reasons for its disappearance. "Let's keep doing what we're doing with the antibiotics and see how you improve in the next few days. Your fever is down and I believe you're on the road to recovery."

I didn't need further explanation. I knew God had answered my prayer. I would get to be a mother for a while longer. Was this a miracle? Believers like me think so. Was it the power of suggestion? Perhaps. Was it all a mistake? Maybe they had misread the first ultrasound? I don't know, nor do I care. I was profoundly grateful I had escaped this crisis and had a chance to see my children grow up. I knew there were no guarantees but I was hopeful as I sailed away from my anniversary year.

I was also tremendously relieved when my oldest daughter, Winnie, moved into her forties, surpassing the death age of her grandmother and great-grandmother, both namesakes of my daughter. Winnie is now fifty with three daughters of her own, just like her great-grandmother. I pray she will live to see them grow up.

Outliving the age of their mother at her death was a goal for some daughters I interviewed. This was true for Beth who I knew through a distant relationship. A family member told me that Beth had lost her mother at an early age so I contacted her about an interview. She agreed and, since she lived nearby, we met at Starbucks. We reminisced about our childhoods as we enjoyed our coffees outside on a sunny day in June.

Beth began the conversation by acknowledging that with a son in college and a daughter planning to leave for college in a year, she was enjoying this time of her life. Leaving the present, Beth then went on to tell her early loss story. She was ten, her mother thirty-four when she died.

Beth's Early Loss Story

"Besides my dad, I had a sister four years older and twin brothers who were eight. We had a housekeeper for a while, but my dad wasn't dealing well with being alone. He remarried five years after my mother died and immersed us into my stepmother's life. Although we got along fairly well, she was very different from my mom.

"My stepmother had two sons, so now we were a family of six children. She worked full time. I was used to a stay-at-home mom who was busy with us kids, crafts, and church. Prior to my dad remarrying, my sister stepped into the role of being my mom. Her intentions were good but her actions strained our relationship as well as her relationship with our stepmom."

When I asked about her anniversary memories, Beth said, "When I reached the age my mother was when she died and realized I would live longer than my mom, I knew I needed a better goal; a bigger, better goal than to simply outlive my mother. I've been working on this."

As our conversation drew to a close, Beth, an easygoing, forty-nine-year-old, summed up her early years and mother loss experience. "I figure there is no point in wondering about the what-ifs. I've always thought that my circumstance of early mother loss didn't make my life better or worse. It just made it different." After Beth surpassed the anniversary of her mother's death, she said she felt renewed purpose and energy for what was next in her life.

Jorie, another daughter of early mother loss and a friend of my son-in-law's, also found the anniversary year to be significant. Jorie, age forty-six, was fourteen when her forty-two-year-old mother died of lung cancer. We spoke on the phone.

Jorie's Early Loss Story

"My mother was a heavy smoker and died of lung cancer. My sister and I helped take care of her when she was sick. During that time she told me to take care of myself, her inference being, 'Don't be dependent upon a man.' Her advice made me gun shy of relationships.

"Within a year of my mother's death, my dad remarried a woman eighteen years younger than he. My mother died in February, by August our stepmom had moved in. Together, they had two daughters so now we were a family of seven girls. My youngest blood sister got lost in it all and I felt compelled to take care of her."

At this point in our conversation, Jorie moved on to talk about her adult life. "Eighteen months after my marriage, I was divorced. Perhaps because of my mother's warning about men, I'm a very independent person. My independence caused tension in our marriage. Also, my mom and dad had not modeled a stable marriage.

"Not having a biological mom influenced me to want a child so, as a single person, I had a daughter. We are very close. Even at seven years old, I allow her a lot of independence."

When asked about her anniversary year, Jorie's voice rose as she emphatically said, "I was aware of it all year, right down to the day. Then I thought to myself, *Wow, this is as far as she went, this is all she got.* It felt incredibly short. Right around that time I put a will together. I kept thinking, *This could be it.* As a single mom, the thought was particularly frightening."

At the end of our conversation, Jorie also confirmed the need to reach out for help early. Jorie said, "I wish I had someone with whom I could have processed my mom's death. I'm not unsettled. However, it would have been helpful to have guidance in pulling the emotional pieces together."

Our imaginations, along with the dread of repeating history, can be very powerful. The cycles of life pull us in directions we might not want to go. This applied to Laura's anniversary experience.

I met Laura online and she chose to email me her story. Laura was nine when her mother died. Laura's maternal grandparents raised her.

Laura's Early Loss Story

I was very close to my grandmother but my grandfather kept his distance. It wasn't until he was very old that he became more present in my life. My grandparents were old fashioned but also loose in their child rearing. Because they were forced into the situation of raising two children, myself and my older sister, I think they turned a blind eye to a lot of things because they didn't want to deal with the issues.

I wasn't close to my sister who completely internalized our mother's death. Although we shared a room, I never saw her cry. Later in life she was diagnosed with schizophrenia. Sometimes I wonder if her lack of processing our mother's death added to her mental illness.

Needing to feel secure and safe, I married an older man with a good job, a house, and aspirations for a family. From the beginning, my husband agreed that I should stay home with the kids rather than work. I knew I would be safe and taken care of. I married a father figure, so to speak.

We have a son and a daughter. I've enjoyed every second of every day being their mother. I've put my heart and soul into parenting and I know now it was as much for me as it was for them. I never wanted my children to have to guess if I loved them. If something took me from them the way my mother was taken from me, I wanted them to know of my love.

Perhaps because of her great love for her children, Laura's anniversary experience was particularly dramatic.

When I reached the anniversary age, I psyched myself out to the point that I thought I had an aneurism just like my mother. I was experiencing incredible headaches that hurt so much I was vomiting. I went to the emergency room and they ran an MRI to check my brain. All was fine except it indicated I had a sinus infection. A sinus infection! I was amazed by what my mind could do. I was also very relieved to not repeat my mother loss history.

Like Laura, we all feel relief as we move past the anniversary year. Ana had some additional advice to impart to daughters. I spoke with Ana on the phone. Ana was twenty-three when her fifty-eight-year-old mother died.

Ana's Young Adult Loss Story

"My Dad and I were both lost after my mother died and I was stressed to the limit. Then, Dad was diagnosed with prostate cancer right after my mother's funeral. I didn't want to be home and experience his illness. I'd had enough. As a result of my need to escape the past and current circumstances, I made bad choices. Actually, I made a mess of my life and didn't really recover until like yesterday—kidding, but not kidding.

"I'm divorced. I believe my parents had a very good marriage and, as a result, I think I had unrealistic marriage expectations. My ex-husband pretty much thought he could do anything and get away with it because I didn't have parents to run home to. Now I have a daughter and I want to make sure she benefits from everything I learned from my marriage experience. I'm very honest about what I've done in the past as I don't want anything to surprise or hurt her down the road if I'm not around to explain it to her."

Ana is also concerned about the possibility of not living a long life.

"Because of my loss experience, I worry about dying young and so does my brother. Because of the tragedy of our parents, my oldest brother, who is sixty-one, thought he would die before he reached sixty. Having lost a mom early has also made me very aware of age but also thankful that I'm still around."

Now, at forty-seven, Ana had some words of wisdom for other daughters. "Remember that your mom's story doesn't have to be your story. Make sure you don't leave anything in your closet, unworn, with the tags on. Finally, don't be mad that your mom's gone, be glad you're still here."

Hope Edelman refers to reaching the age your mother died as the "magic number." In her book, *Motherless Daughters: The Legacy of Loss*, she writes, "This can be a time of both sadness and rebirth. The daughter fears leaving her mother behind—and many feel guilty for seeing years her mother never got to see—but also feels relief that her destiny will differ from her mother's."

Research suggests that the parents' longevity doesn't correlate directly with the longevity of their children. James Vaupel of the Max Planck Institute for Demographic Research in Rostock, Germany, is quoted at sharpbrains. com as saying, "Inheritance has surprisingly little influence on longevity. Only six percent of how long you'll live, compared with the average, is explained by your parents' longevity. By contrast, up to ninety percent of how tall you are is explained by your parents' height. Even genetically identical twins vary widely in life span: the typical gap is more than fifteen years."

If you have not yet reached your anniversary year, write that quote down and post it to your fridge. Perhaps it will not quell your fearful emotions, but facts are powerful tools in our arsenal of recovery and well-being. Learn to reinforce the positive, affirm what is now, and resist making assumptions.

If your mother died of dementia, the outlook around inheritance is a bit different. There is a hereditary component to Alzheimer's. Dr. Nathan Hermann, a memory disorders specialist, writes in YourHealthMatters, "In terms of risk for family members, it is important to know that there are two types of Alzheimer's disease. A very rare form of the illness, referred to as 'Familial Alzheimer's disease,' occurs in only about two per cent of individuals with the illness and has been linked with three genetic mutations involving chromosomes 21, 1 and 14.

"In this form of the illness, there is a fifty percent chance of developing the disease if you have a parent with a confirmed genetic mutation. The other disturbing aspect of this illness is that—unlike the more common form of Alzheimer's disease that typically begins in a person's 70s and 80s—this form of the illness can begin as early as in a person's 40s and 50s."

Dr. Hermann goes on to write, "Most people who develop Alzheimer's disease have what is called 'Sporadic Alzheimer's disease.' If your mother had this disease, your risk of developing the illness is about two to three times higher than someone else your age who doesn't have a family member with the illness."

For daughters whose mothers have, or had, Alzheimer's, the anniversary they are concerned about isn't expressed in an exact year but as a life stage. These daughters look at the their own aging through the lens of their mother loss experience. For instance, as they approach the age of their mother when she was diagnosed with Alzheimer's, they may become hypersensitive to forgetfulness or loss of focus. During this time, it is important for them to reassure themselves that they are not their mother. According to the Alzheimer's Association, although the risk to daughters of mothers diagnosed with Alzheimer's may be heightened, they can improve their chances of not developing the disease by eating a healthy diet, staying socially active, avoiding tobacco and excess alcohol, and exercising both body and mind.

The Alzheimer's Association web site states that the greatest risk factor for Alzheimer's disease is advancing age. Most individuals with the disease are age sixty-five or older. The likelihood of developing Alzheimer's doubles about every five years after age sixty-five. After age eighty-five, the risk reaches nearly fifty percent. These statistics make the anniversary of a mother's decline and eventual death from Alzheimer's even more daunting than if she had died from another disease.

Maria Shriver founded the Women's Alzheimer's Movement after her father, Sargent Shriver, died of the disease. Her website states, "Every sixty-six seconds a new brain develops Alzheimer's. Two-thirds of them belong to women. At sixty years old, a woman is twice as likely to develop Alzheimer's disease than breast cancer."

Gina is one of the daughters I interviewed who is looking at her future through the lens of having a mother with Alzheimer's. The director of a memory care unit, with whom I was acquainted, referred Gina to me. As we spoke on the phone, Gina used the phrase, "twice lost" in reference to losing her eighty-six-year-old mother to Alzheimer's disease.

Gina's Alzheimer's Loss Story

"I've lost her now and I know I'll lose her yet again with her passing. This double loss is heart wrenching. Four years ago, after my stepfather died, I began noticing changes in my mother. For instance, one time she left the car running in the garage. Another day, I found pizza in the oven left from the night before. She became lost while driving. I think my stepdad took care to mask what was happening, but after he died and her condition became apparent, we immediately sought a neurologist. It wasn't long before she was in a memory care unit."

Just four years later, Gina considers her mother, as she knew her, to be gone. "Now my mother is my baby. She can't remember her name, can't have a conversation, her once meticulous silver hair is disheveled. In the beginning I lost patience when she forgot things. I regret this. Now I want to go back and savor those times."

Gina admitted that it's hard to see healthy mothers and daughters together including her own mother-in-law who is still a vibrant woman. Gina also worries about her own future. She considers who might take care of her if she develops Alzheimer's. Although she has two sons and a husband, she still wonders, knowing how difficult it is, how they would deal with a wife or mother succumbing to dementia. Gina said she considers her "anniversary" a possible unknown date in the future when she could become a baby like her mother.

Marti is another daughter who considers her future in light of her mother dying of Alzheimer's. A close personal friend, Marti is a pert, seventy-four-year-old retired nurse who gladly shared her story with me.

Marti's Alzheimer's Loss Story

"My mother and I were very close. She was quite social and had many friends before she lost her ability to carry on a conversation. In the beginning, when we talked on the phone, she could hide her failing memory. Rather than talking and, thereby, revealing herself, she encouraged me to talk by asking questions. This worked well for her until, at her granddaughter's wedding, when she was handed the microphone to say a few words, she didn't know what to do with it. We knew then, even before we had an actual diagnosis, that she was starting the slow downhill slide."

After her mother dropped out of everything social, she began phoning Marti more frequently. Marti didn't object. "I knew she was lonely and bored. She had lost her ability to read and focus on television in addition to being isolated from her friends.

"As the disease progressed, I dreaded going to visit my mother, as she was not herself—not my mother. We were fortunate that she never wandered, as many folks do, and she was never mean. Although she was very upset when we moved her to a nursing home, she quickly forgot that she had been moved."

Marti continued by discussing her mother's death and her recommendations for others. "In the end, death was a relief. She was a body without a functioning brain. There was much grieving before her death as it was a very gradual loss."

Marti advised people who have parents with severe dementia to seek respite care for the caregivers. "Remember, the caregiver has few social interactions. They are with a person day and night who can't share memories, has no time orientation, who may be difficult to move into an activity, or even take for a ride. Caregivers are often considered the invisible second patient. Self care is critical."

I asked Marti what her thoughts were concerning her own future health. "My mother didn't start to show signs of the disease until she was in her mid-eighties but I've already made plans. My husband and three adult daughters know my specific wishes regarding my care. I have my papers in order including a will, a living will, a medical power of attorney, an advanced directive, and a do not resuscitate (DNR) order.

"Although I know the statistics and, I must admit, I do have a heightened awareness when I can't remember things, I don't dwell on the anniversary of the onset of my mother showing signs of Alzheimer's. Instead, I work to stay healthy which includes getting plenty of exercise."

Anniversaries and other milestone years or events can catch us off guard if we don't anticipate their possible impact. They can also serve as growth opportunities, a time to bring our past and present life into focus and celebrate who we have become.

Now What?

If you have not yet reached the age your mother was when she died or was swept up by dementia, take care to not be blindsided by the anniversary and its significance. Be ready, not with a mind filled with anxiety, but with facts and the assurance that you can survive and thrive past this auspicious date or season in time.

Coaching Questions

- How did the anniversary of turning your mother's age when she died impact you? If you have not yet reached the anniversary year, how do you foresee it impacting you?

- How did/will you cope with these feelings? If you have not yet reached the anniversary age, to whom can you reach out for support when the time comes?

- If your mother suffered from dementia, what will you do to prepare yourself for your own aging?

- What are other important milestones in your life? How might they be affected by your mother loss experience?

STEP FOUR

GET CREATIVE

The discipline of creation, be it to paint,
compose, write, is an effort toward wholeness.
—Madeleine L'engle, author

If you're grieving, you may feel like most things in your life have changed. Returning to or discovering your creativity can be a comforting and familiar friend during this time of your life. If you're a naturally creative person, return to your favorite creative endeavor. If creativity is new to you, consider adding an accessible, achievable activity to your life.

A creative project, even one as simple as coloring, can be a focus and something you can look forward to. During the anxious early months of the COVID-19 pandemic, I turned to coloring to help me relax and forget the world for awhile. Doing something creative can also be a channel to improve your self-esteem. Many creative endeavors like painting, photography, or writing will give you an outlet for your feelings and emotions.

Katherine Parrott, creativity coach, writer, artist, and photographer who helps soulful women unlock their creative genius, writes, "Creativity is a portal into joy. No matter your age, stage, ability, or creative outlet, creativity gives you a place to simply be, to turn up, and either feel all there is to feel, or lose yourself entirely in the creative process."

My dad modeled creativity for me and I believe he likely used it as part of his healing process and as a way to relieve the stress of raising a little girl. With a love of wood, my father made plates, bowls, candle holders—anything round and wood—on a lathe. It was a lifelong hobby he learned from his father. Perhaps because of this modeling, creativity has always played an important role in my life. I didn't associate my early creative endeavors like sewing, knitting, poetry writing, wall art, cooking, or gardening with healing but now I know there was a connection.

My Creative Story

One of the first connections I consciously made between creativity and moving forward after mother loss, was when I turned fifty while I was participating in a therapy group. To celebrate this milestone birthday, my therapist and group leader, Barbra McCoy Getz, LCSW, had a Croning Ceremony for me. Through this ceremony, Barbra encouraged me to consider how becoming a crone or, Wise Woman, could be a positive experience.

Barbra also used the ceremony to help me get in touch with my memories and feelings concerning mother loss. To do this, she asked me to prepare a memorial service for my mother as part of my ceremony. She wanted me to share my mother-memories with the group and write a letter to my mother. Her assignment was a surprise and a challenge. I hadn't tied my mother into this time of my life other than to be grateful that I'd outlived her by sixteen years. The creative assignment felt significant and I followed through. In fact, many of the memories shared in this book came from the work I did at that time.

At Barbra's request, I wore a floppy straw hat with a purple flower and a shawl to set the stage. Part of the ceremony involved breaking a stick. Each half of the stick made a path through which I ceremonially stepped into the next phase of my life. I felt a renewal of positive energy as I accepted the mantle of Wise Woman. I shared my mother-memories as requested, brought a vase of pink carnations in memory of my mother's funeral, and received lovely little gifts that a mother might give a daughter, such as a tiny china tea set. I also wrote and shared the following letter to my mother.

July 1995

Dear Mom,

On this advent of turning 50 years old, I want to remember you and thank you for giving me life. I know the circumstances of my birth were difficult for you. I wish you had had a mother to support you.

As motherless daughters, maybe we both struggled with this mothering business. I'm not sure we received the love we needed and, subsequently, I'm not sure we were able to fully love. I'm grateful that the chain of early death has been broken and my daughters and son have a mother through their growing up years.

I've missed you many times in my life, especially for the big events and, even now, whenever I'm sick. I wish you had been there to fuss over me when I attended dances and when I was married. I wish you could have known and spoiled your grandchildren.

Thank you for marrying such a wonderful man. He has always been a great father to me. I know he loved you very much. I'm sorry you had to leave this earth at such a young age. Sorry for you and sorry for me. I've always remembered that your last words before you died were of me and your wish for me to grow up to become a wonderful woman. I think I have not disappointed you.

I wish you were here now as I step into a new arena of womanhood. I wish you could tell me what it's like to be an "older" woman. I wish we could be friends. I need a best friend like you. I bet we could have fun together and fill a room with love and laughter.

Your daughter,

Mershon (I'm glad you picked this name, I've loved it over the years)

The creativity involved in this Croning Ceremony, including sharing my mother memories and writing this letter, was a turning point in understanding the impact of my early loss. It was the first time I expressed my feelings in a concrete way and shared them with others. In addition, the ceremony set me on a path to becoming the Wise Woman I aspired to be. Later that year, I facilitated Croning Ceremonies for other women and set out on a path to becoming a Certified Personal/Professional Coach.

Monica, a daughter with a traumatic mother loss experience, also turned to writing as a vehicle to begin healing and making sense of her loss. I met Monica, twenty-six years old when we spoke on the phone, in a mother loss support group. At the beginning of our conversation, Monica said she believes there was no violence between her mother and her birth father. When she was two years old, however, her parents divorced and her mother remarried. Monica's stepfather murdered her mother on May 31, 2000, but Monica said her mother loss story began much earlier.

Monica's Homicide Story

"Even at a young age, my instincts told me there was something wrong in my family. It turned out later that my instincts about the arguments, tension, control, and fear were correct.

"As young as four I began to realize there was really terrible abuse going on, which usually involved weapons. My stepfather was a Chicago police officer at the time.

"Later, while my stepfather spent four years in prison for trafficking drugs, my mom changed and became more confident and self-reliant. When I started fifth grade, my stepfather returned from prison and my mom allowed him back into our lives. However, my mom soon moved us out, yet again, and we spent nine months in an apartment. The following January she returned to him for the third time and she was murdered in May. At the time of her death, she was preparing to move again.

"When my stepfather discovered she had withdrawn money from their account, he sensed that this time she would not return. She had grown stronger and he realized that she no longer loved him. I believe these were the triggers that caused him to murder her."

Monica took a breath before continuing with the details of her story.

"My mom, brother, and I were just returning from church. I asked to be dropped off at my boyfriend's and my brother went to a friend's house. When my brother and I returned home, no one was in the house. We called our mom and stepdad but no one answered. Later in the evening, my stepfather appeared at the door but we didn't let him in because he looked wild and he seemed to be in a panic. That night I stayed at my aunt's house in order to feel safe. Later, my mom's car was found parked in front of my brother's friend's house with her body in the trunk. I immediately suspected my stepdad."

After the police arrested her stepfather, Monica, only seventeen at the time, lived with her birth father for a few months. "I moved out when I discovered my dad and my mom's two sisters withheld and spent money my mom intended for my siblings and me. Next, I moved in with my boyfriend's family. It was such a relief to live with them. They gave me support and helped me make plans for college. Although, I had previously considered college and knew my mom wanted me to go, I knew nothing about financial aid and loans until this family encouraged me."

Finding justice for this tragedy was a long, drawn-out ordeal. "When the case went to court, there were constant delays due to my stepfather changing attorneys. There were four different lawyers and each one needed time to get up to speed on the case. It dragged on for nine years. I think the strategy was to play a psychological game in order to exhaust both the family and the judge. My stepfather declined to take the stand and never shed a tear. All he said to my brother and me was, 'It was my loss too.' Today he is in prison."

After Monica's initial grief lifted, she began to realize what life was like without her mother. "I had nightmares, flashbacks, and PTSD. I went to therapy to help me cope. However, after my brothers and I got through the worst of it, my mom's death became a huge motivator for us. I went to college and became a mental health case manager. Now, I'm a writer, domestic violence advocate, and a personal trainer. My brothers and I are doing great. Our mother's death gave us a higher purpose."

Monica wrote *The Third Return: A Memoir*. The title comes from the fact that her mother left then returned three times to Monica's stepfather.

"Writing a book about my mother's life and death helped me in my recovery. As I wrote, I had to better understand my mother's perspective and why she made the decisions she did. It was hard discovering some things about her but I came to accept that she was a person with flaws just like us all.

"When I learn that my writing influences and touches the lives of others, I feel more joy than I ever imagined."

Monica believes that although it's tempting to engage in destructive coping strategies, it is important to find creative outlets. More information about Monica and her writing, including her statement to the court, can be found on her website, www.youbeautifullife.com.

The next story is how Annette, who was diagnosed with early-onset Alzheimer's, and her daughter, Allie, also used writing to help them cope.

As difficult as it is at any age to lose a mother to Alzheimer's, losing a mother to this disease and becoming a caregiver when you are still a child yourself is an experience with its own set of trials. I met Annette's family through a mutual friend. Annette, a victim of early-onset Alzheimer's, was diagnosed at age forty-seven. At the time of her diagnosis, her daughters were nine and eleven.

Annette's response to her early onset diagnosis can be put into perspective through the words of fantasy author, Terry Pratchett who, before he died of early onset Alzheimer's in 2015, was quoted in the *Naples Daily News* as saying, "It occurred to me that at one point it was like I had two diseases—one was Alzheimer's and the other was knowing I had Alzheimer's."

Three years into her life with Alzheimer's, Annette used writing to help her deal with the two diseases to which Pratchett refers. Although Annette's cognitive abilities were somewhat impaired at the time of writing, her words give us insight into the mind of a person on the journey.

Annette's Early-Onset Alzheimer's Story Written In Her Words

"Living with Alzheimer's" by Annette La Spisa Wheat (Fifty years old at time of writing)

Since my diagnosis and now living with Alzheimer's, I find I am dependent on people to bring me food and, hopefully, a variety and not the same kind over and over.

People need to take me out so I am not always homebound. People need to take me to purchase clothes. My clothes dwindle after a while and some are different sizes or out of style, even shoes. I do not get to go out and exercise the way I used to. At times I actually go upstairs and downstairs in my house in order to just get some exercise. I know that the number one statistic for women is having heart attacks and I do not want this on top of Alzheimer's. No more going swimming, which I miss. No more going dancing. I feel the loss of these things and the feeling of isolation especially in the winter months. I even have to see if I can have someone that is going to church bring me with. I miss driving and going to plays. Another loss is my independence.

I feel my spouse does not show affection—hugs, kisses, no intimacy at all, and yet I am still capable of this. I receive excuses as to why there is no intimacy. I now have a caregiver but not the same husband. My spouse thinks there are a lot of things I cannot do and yet wants to get a second dog.

I have concern over my kids that, as they grow up, they will want to help me but I still want them to be kids and not become my caregivers at such young ages. Instead of them trying to take control over some things in the house, I wish they would ask what I need. One child is neutral and takes care of herself, plus gets good grades.

My best friend these days is Bella my dog. My greatest gift is my mother.

I have not entertained in my home for over one year now since having Alzheimer's. There are days that I am not sure of the time and date. When it gets dark early, I am not sure of the season.

Since I have developed Alzheimer's I feel I no longer have girlfriends. I used to have friends but they no longer come around or even call.

My feelings get hurt when my spouse or child comes up to me and smells my hair and asks, "When was the last time you took a shower or washed your hair?"

Three years after Annette wrote this narrative, she was moved to a memory care facility.

I spoke with Allie, Annette's oldest daughter, seven years after her mother's Alzheimer's diagnosis. Allie was eighteen when we spoke over the phone. Her mother was in memory care and still recognized her but had difficulty carrying on a conversation. As you can imagine, life was challenging for this young woman, especially when her mother was living at home when Allie was between the ages eleven to eighteen.

Allie's Alzheimer's Loss Story

"I didn't invite friends to the house when my mom was still at home because I was embarrassed by how she looked and acted. I bombed in school because I had so much to do including the dishes and cleaning the house. My mom wanted to be independent but she couldn't be.

"Finally, at the beginning of my senior year, she was placed in memory care. We spent six years living at home with her. I felt resentful. I had missed participating in clubs and sports and my schoolwork had suffered. I began to see my mom as a little sister yet, in many ways, she was still my mom—it was very confusing."

To give me a glimpse of her life when her mother lived at home, Allie told me about her mother's driving experiences. "When my mother was still driving, I often accompanied her in the car in case she became confused or lost. Once in a while I even drove, although I was only twelve at the time. My family knew this was illegal, but occasionally, it was the only solution we had.

"Prior to me learning to drive and accompanying my mother, we had this experience: One day my mom set out by herself to take my younger sister to school, which was just a short distance away. Two hours after dropping Rachel off at school, she returned home with a pie from Wisconsin. We live in a suburb of Chicago. It's a miracle she finally found her way home."

During the time her mother was still at home, Allie went to therapy for eight months. "I loved it. It was wonderful to talk to an understanding person about what was going on in my life. My sister wouldn't go and I think that someday she will regret that decision. Another support in my life is my best friend whose mom has schizophrenia. She understands what real problems are. I used to get really upset when friends talked about little things that they considered to be big problems."

To help her cope with her feelings during her caregiving years, Allie tapped into the creative experience of writing poetry. The first poem she wrote was for a poetry competition when she was a high school junior. She won, and her poem was included in a school publication.

"Know Her" by Alexandra Wheat

All who meet her love her
Little do they know the real her
Zoo animals can remember more
Her eyes always filled with confusion
Early onset they call it
I can see the real her
Mood swings are the least of our problems
Everyone says I have her beautiful face
Running out the door is her only escape
She is lost in the blink of an eye

Depression swallows her
I can see the real her
She cries herself to sleep
Every night I put a smile on her face
Annette is the best she can be
Soon our time will end
Everyone will know the real her

This second poem was written about a year later.

"Don't You Forget About Me" by Allie Wheat

I cannot say the words, they are too hard to say
I rue the moment that I fade, the memories went away
I had a beautiful mom whose mind went one day
I had a mom who was too sick to stay
I blame the disease that stripped her that way
I hate that I won't see her on my wedding day
I feel the pain of her suffering, I carry it everyday
I hate when people assume she is fine, she looks okay

I just need her back, please only today
I know it's selfish, but I pray
I only have the memories in my head set on replay
I miss her arms around me, was it just yesterday
I wasted our time, begging to go play
I missed all the stories from back in the day
I have the pictures and the perfume you over-sprayed
I found the strength to take it day by day
I will see you again Mom, someday.

Allie found that poetry was an acceptable way of expressing her feelings at a time when emotions ran high in her family. As she was struggling with containing her anger, fear, disappointment, and sadness, poetry gave her an outlet for her emotions.

In addition to writing poetry, being part of the documentary, *Too Soon To Forget: Supporting Those with Younger Onset Alzheimer's Disease* was also healing for Allie. "Being honest about how I felt and continue to feel, has been very powerful. The documentary made our life situation public but it also made it possible for us to help others."

TMK Productions produced *Too Soon to Forget* with support from the Rush Alzheimer's Disease Center. The RADC is recognized around the world as a leader in Alzheimer's research and treatment. The documentary stresses the need for community involvement and support including: family, friends, neighbors, clergy, and professionals. With younger-onset Alzheimer's, families are challenged with maintaining careers, caregiving, financial considerations, and the care of younger children.

Allie says her grandmother, Jean, keeps the family stable. "She is always there for us, she is a rock in our lives. Some of the rest of the family just don't understand and are not there for us. My grandmother has been a true mother figure."

At the time of our interview, Allie was a full-time college student and working part-time. "I feel like I have my life back. Although it is heartbreaking to know what is happening to my mom, my life is moving forward in a positive way. My sister, who is in high school, is getting to do all the things I missed and is a great student. I'm happy for her."

In addition to sharing Allie's happiness for her sister, I'm also happy for Allie. Although she's living through an experience no teen or young adult should have to endure, she is thriving.

Daughters like Allie and others seem to benefit from their creative endeavors in a variety of ways. Sometimes creativity helps them express their feelings, other times it forges a path for their life's work like Sarah who turned her creative endeavors into a career.

I went to college with Sarah's mother who died at fifty-six of breast cancer. Sarah was twenty-one and finishing her junior year in college when her mother died. We were reconnected by a mutual friend and spoke on the phone.

Sarah's Young Adult Loss Story

"My mother first had cancer in 1985 when I was five or six. She recovered and was in remission for ten years. She became sick again in 1996 and fought the disease for five years. By then the cancer had metastasized to her bones. I always wondered, *What would my life have been like if mom had died when I was only five?* It was a shadow of reality for me and I wondered if it was the same for my mom. I have always been in touch with the idea that life might not be long."

Sarah continued by talking about what life was like after her mother died. "My dad was an alcoholic and we had a challenging relationship. I returned to school after my mother's death, graduated, and moved to another state. Twenty-one is a time of transition into adulthood. My mom and I were just becoming friends and we were very close. With her death it felt like my whole childhood kind of vanished. I still miss her presence, her friendship, my feeling of being safe in the world. I've not had the same feeling of safety since her death. I still miss her in every way. As I've aged, my loss has become more clear."

I too have recognized the significance of my mother loss as I've aged. Becoming a grandmother and seeing my grandchildren at the age I was when my mother died gave me new insight into how young and vulnerable I was at eight years old. I didn't see this as clearly when my children were growing up. Perhaps I was too busy being a parent. As a grandmother, I have more time to reflect and I'm more mature and introspective.

Becoming a mother set Sarah back on her heels for a while. "I was a premature baby and when my daughter was also born prematurely at twenty-eight weeks, weighing one pound thirteen ounces, the experience broke the scab off my mother loss recovery. Our birth experiences would have been so bonding."

Sarah recently published a book about premature birth experiences, which has a memoir component to it. Writing the book, *Early: An Intimate History of Premature Birth and What It Teaches Us About Being Human* is another way Sarah used her talent and creativity to heal.

"My mom was a children's librarian and loved her job. It was very important to her. She called it her 'dream job.' She hoped that I too would be lucky enough to have work that fed my soul. When Mom died I asked myself, *What can I do to make myself happy? What would Mom have wanted?* I decided I wanted to share her value of doing work she loved.

"One of my mom's great gifts to me was the love of books. By giving me the love of books and writing, my mom gave me what I needed to survive without her and be happy. I am a journalist and I love my work."

Loving her work has translated into success. Sarah is a James Beard Award nominated freelance food writer, editor, and recipe developer. She's been a staff food editor at *Food & Wine, Parade,* and *Food Network Magazine.* Her work has appeared in the *New York Times, The Wall Street Journal,* and *Martha Stewart Living* to name a few.

"My creative endeavors helped me not only move forward but to continue my mom's legacy of loving my work."

When I asked Sarah what advice she had for other daughters, she said, "I'm still figuring it out. I think it's okay that the hole in your heart never leaves you. You learn to live with it. When my mother first died, I thought of Crater Lake in south central Oregon as an analogy. It's the deepest lake in the United States and I imagine that this lake is in my body. As a symbol of my mother loss, I feel as if I'm always walking around it."

Like Sarah, it seems many daughters have found that tapping into their creativity can change their perspective.

Perhaps it helps them give up the identity of victim or grieving daughter as they take up the new identity of writer, dancer, or musician.

Andrea Rosenhaft, a writer and Licensed Clinical Social Worker, who spent her late twenties and thirties battling anorexia, major depression, and borderline personality disorder wrote in her blog entitled, *From Both Sides of the Couch,* "I realized that I didn't need cocaine or cutting, starving or fantasizing about suicide to experience a high. The process of writing, of putting words down on paper, of finding my rhythm with language—this was a very different kind of high. It was better. It was enduring."Although Andrea wasn't dealing with mother loss, I've included her quote because I believe it's a powerful statement by someone "on both sides of the couch" about the healing powers of writing.

Creativity can take you in many directions. In addition to writing books, consider writing entries in a diary, journal, or blogging. Try your hand at short stories or hand-written letters to people you care about. Pick up a pencil, glue stick, or paint brush. Try doodling, drawing, painting, coloring, card making, or scrapbooking. Buy yourself some needles and a pattern and start knitting or crocheting. Get your hands dirty with woodworking, furniture refinishing, or gardening. Use your musical abilities by singing in a choir or playing an instrument. Take cooking lessons and whip up something delectable. Anything you enjoy that puts you in touch with your creative side will help you move forward in your journey.

If you engage in a creative activity you truly enjoy, you may get into the state of flow—a feeling of being so completely engaged in an activity that you lose your sense of self and time. Flow reduces anxiety, boosts your mood, and even slows your heart rate. When you create something that gives you pleasure, your brain is flooded with the feel-good chemical, dopamine. As I pursue my favorite creative activities like writing, cooking, gardening, and singing in a choir, I experience reduced anxiety and stress. Some women I spoke with who were still in the grieving process, felt less depressed when they engaged in their favorite creative endeavor.

Now What?

Take the fourth step of your journey by tapping into your creativity. Discover your creative outlet and begin to express yourself. While making a difference in your ability to move forward, tapping into your creativity may also bring you a renewed sense of joy.

Coaching Questions

- What creative outlet will you use to help you cope with your loss? What sounds like fun?

- How might engaging in this creative activity help you move forward?

- If you're feeling resistant to expressing yourself in a creative way, what do you think is holding you back?

—⊱✿⊰—

SPRING OPEN THE GUILT AND SECRECY TRAP

*The causes of familial discord and distance are
countless, the results are often the same: secrecy, blame,
sadness, hurt, confusion, and feelings of loss and grief.*

—Sharon Salzburg, author of
Real Love: The Art of Mindful Connection

Research shows that feelings of guilt and a sense of secrecy
are common among daughters who have experienced
mother loss. Let's start with the situations that may cause
guilty feelings. If a mother died when a daughter was a teenager, she may have been in the midst of a difficult, push-pull
relationship and she now feels guilty that she wasn't more
cooperative or respectful.

Perhaps the daughter was a busy mother or working
woman when her mother was sick and now the daughter
feels guilty about not spending more quality time with
her mother. Those who were young when their mothers
died may feel guilty about not remembering what their
mother looked like, how she sounded, or her favorite
food. An abandoned daughter can be angry and have

guilt over not moving on from her experience or being unable to forgive.

Caregivers may harbor resentment, not only toward their mother for becoming incapable of caring for herself, but toward other family members who didn't step up emotionally, physically or financially to help at a difficult time. As a result, these daughters may feel guilty about their resentment. Daughters of murdered mothers may have guilt about their anger toward their mothers for putting themselves in harm's way.

Acknowledging and recognizing one's guilt and it's source is a good first step towards resolution. Daughters need to come to terms with their feelings if they're to spring open the trap and set themselves free.

In his book, *Grief is a Journey*, Dr. Kenneth J. Doka describes several types of guilt following the death or extreme decline of a loved one. Dr. Doka explains that for young daughters, grief guilt can surface if they feel guilty or ashamed about how poorly they are coping with their loss. Doka writes, "Young girls may see their siblings and father moving on with their lives and wonder why they are stuck in an overwhelming sadness. Having no one with whom they can express their grief, they become increasing guilty that they have not moved on and they wonder what is wrong with them."

Doka also writes about recovery guilt, the feeling that we are doing too well. Katie, who shared her story of the murder of her mother by her stepfather, said that she experiences this guilt as she strives to recover normalcy in her life. "When I feel guilty about feeling good I tell myself this is a normal reaction and I try to embrace the joy, not the guilt."

Causation guilt is guilt felt by daughters who think that somehow their mother died or left them because of their own actions. These young women think, *If only I had been a better daughter my mother would not have died.* Or, *If only I hadn't said those cruel words or stayed home more or loved her more, etc., she would still be here.*

Moral guilt can be experienced by those who believe that the sins of the fathers will be visited on their children. Daughters may believe that their mother's death or suffering or their own suffering is the result of a sinful family.

The opposite side of this guilty coin can be survivor's pride. Maxine Harris, Ph.D., author of *The Loss That Is Forever*, writes, "In the final stage of successful mourning, children come to see loss and their ability to survive as part of the same tapestry. Rather than feeling overwhelmed by grief and despair, they are aware of their own strength to manage adversity."

Discovering one's strength through adversity is an important part of the journey. This awareness can serve us throughout our lives. The following is a visual metaphor for this healing process. In Japan, broken objects are often repaired with gold. The flaw is seen as a unique piece of the object's history, adding to its beauty. A green vase with a large crack repaired with gold is a lovely visual. Rather than hidden, the crack is accentuated by the gold, giving the vase character and a beautiful design. Often, the repaired vase is even stronger than it was in its original form.

Wouldn't it be wonderful if we could visualize our lives like this vase? Rather than hiding, concealing, and feeling guilty about the cracks or brokenness in our lives—our losses, our mistakes, our injuries—we could turn them into something beautiful and useful like renewed resilience, greater empathy, or strength of character. Like the gold streak in the vase, however, no matter how well we recover, our experience of loss will always be a part of our lives or, as Harris writes, "When a parent dies young, the experience of loss and the creation of self are forever merged."

Secrecy is another common denominator. In some families, the disease or circumstances that took the mother's life are never mentioned and photos of the mother are put away. Whether by mutual consent or by authoritarian declaration, the family does not discuss the loss nor the cause of the loss. The unspoken agreement is, "Don't ask, don't tell," where everyone is expected to act as if nothing happened. Some motherless daughters who grew up in an environment of secrecy felt that the secrecy seriously compounded the issue of their mother's death.

I recently read a story of a teenage daughter whose mother waited until a year after her diagnosis to tell her daughter about her breast cancer. The mother explained that she didn't tell her daughter earlier because she didn't want her to worry. The daughter felt angry, hurt, and shaken. "I felt like an afterthought and wondered if my mom thought I was this fragile child who couldn't handle anything critical even though I was sixteen-years-old."

Later, the daughter wondered if she was that incapable. "The thought laid seeds of doubt in my brain." The daughter reported that even as an adult she sometimes feels paralyzed by stressful situations and questions her ability to get through them. The damaging result of secrets can last a lifetime.

My friend Wendy's story illustrates the extreme side of secrecy. Wendy, seventy-four, grew up in Canada. We met in a cooking group called "Smoking Pots" where we shared a love of cooking, reading, and all things about Julia Child. She told me her mother loss story in person.

Wendy's Early Loss Story

"My mother died when I was fifteen. I received the bad news while I was on a school trip to Venice, Italy. I was devastated and didn't know how to process this information. I always had the strong hope and belief that something would happen to make her better. I was not privy to any information regarding a funeral service and still to this day don't know exactly what happened except she was cremated and her ashes were strewn around Lake Tremblant in the Laurentian Mountains where we had a summer home. She was a brilliant and beautiful and highly accomplished woman."

Wendy continues by talking about the history of secrecy that preceded her mother's death.

"I actually lost my mother five years earlier when she was taken from our home to the Verdun Mental Hospital and never returned. I wasn't allowed to visit her, to speak to her, or to speak of her illness."

I felt shock and dismay when Wendy told me this. It seemed unimaginable to me that a young daughter was not allowed to see or speak of her mother while she was still alive. I asked Wendy to explain.

"My mother had Pick's Disease, a rare neurological degeneration disease similar to Alzheimer's. It is a very fast form of dementia with no possible recovery. It was my father's decision to keep me from visiting my mother in the hospital because he felt she was too unstable. My father was a general surgeon. He was very cold and forbade complaining or whining. He said, 'Suck it up, no one cares about your feelings.' My mother, on the other hand, was warm and loving. She was an amazing woman. Losing her the way I did left a terrible hole in my life.

"To compound my loss, soon after my mom entered the hospital, my father went to the Canadian Arctic for a year to do research. He was a brilliant physician and in the forefront of medical technology. While he was away, an aunt came to care for my two siblings and me. She was the aunt that my parents referred to by saying, 'If you're not good, we'll send you to live with Auntie Ruth.' Now Auntie Ruth had come to live with us. She was not a loving person.

"My mother's health was a big family secret. The worst thing that could happen was if someone found out about my mother. My best friend, with whom I had sleepovers, was the only friend who knew my mom was in the hospital. Of course, I didn't know that my mother would never return home. Mostly, no one even knew my mom was gone, much less in the hospital. The secrecy felt like a weight on us all. The sadness of having my mother gone was compounded by the stress of constantly living a secret life."

Luckily, Wendy had Phyllis, a childless family friend who knew her circumstances and who took her under her wing so that she had some love and support as she was growing up.

Wendy took a breath before she continued with the story of the years following her mother's death.

"My mother died the end of July and that fall I was sent away to boarding school. I only came home for Christmas. I absolutely despised being there. I think I was probably also depressed.

"A couple of years before my mother died, my father frequently spoke about a colleague, Doctor So and So. Later, we were surprised to learn this colleague was a woman doctor. My father married her right after my mother died. She wanted her own heirs so they had two sons. I have very little contact with these stepbrothers. I do have contact with my siblings but we are not close. I have two siblings, a sister who is five years older, and a brother three and a half years older."

I know Wendy to be a joy-filled, successful, thriving woman. I asked her how this came about given her dark childhood. "As cold as my father was, he instilled a solid work ethic in me. He'd say, 'Work hard and learn to take care of yourself.' I took his advice."

Wendy has a Bachelor's Degree in Music, a Master's in Library and Information Science, and a Doctorate in Instructional Technology. She taught in the graduate school of Information and Library Science at Southern Connecticut State University for thirty-five years.

"My first marriage ended in divorce. We were married for nine years. If my mother had been alive, I believe I wouldn't have left Montreal and I wouldn't have married someone I didn't love. I was twenty-one years old and wanted to get away. I couldn't think of any reason not to marry him.

"Although I've been happily together with my second husband, Bob, for forty years, I think losing my mother initially made me think, *I'm not going to love anyone again as I don't want to suffer like I did when I lost my mother.*

"One reason I've been able to thrive is I learned to look for growth possibilities and people with whom I could share ideas and experiences. Even though I had an early life shrouded in secrecy that caused me emotional pain, I rebounded into having a rich and full adult life."

Although I don't know what motivated Wendy's father to keep his wife's illness a secret, I do know that guilt and shame are frequently the cause. Some families feel judged in their inability to care for a sick loved one, they may have shame that a perceived family weakness brought on the disease and subsequent death, or they feel shame about being different. I believe that to combat these scenarios, families need to have open discussions that answer all questions about the cause of death, the reason for abandonment, the type of mental illness, and the possible genetics related to a disease. Even the most basic questions from the youngest child need to be addressed and the sharing of memories welcomed by their loved ones.

Wendy's childhood was darkened by her father's adamant command about keeping an "inside" or "family-only" secret.

Sometimes the reverse is true when the outside world knows what's happening in a family but a child is kept in the dark. According to therapists such as Evan Imber-Black, PhD author of *The Secret Life of Families*, not trusting children with the truth breeds fear and resentment rather than love and support, which can, over time, permanently taint a parent-child relationship. While parents may think they're protecting their children from pain by keeping them in the dark, that can actually do more harm than good — to everyone involved. Columbia University researchers studied the effects of 13,000 secrets and found keeping them often led to preoccupation, decreased trust, and reduced satisfaction with life.

In addition to secrets, when language is vague about mother loss, a young daughter may make untrue assumptions.

Saying, "she is gone" or "passed away" or "God needed her" confuses a child and delays the inevitable truth that their mother died and will never return. In my personal experience, and from what I've learned from others, being clear about why a mother died and that she is not coming back, can help a daughter gain trust and the feeling of being worthy enough to hear the hard truths. In keeping the truth away from a grieving child, family members often think they are being gentle and kind when, in fact, they frequently cause the child to be suspicious of future communication and the lack of information leaves them speculating.

Evan Imber-Black, an expert on family secrets, concurs. "You want to help keep life normal in an abnormal situation. [But] stay open to children's questions. While it may feel strange at first, letting your children comfort you is not only okay but encouraged. Keeping something as life-changing as a serious illness from your children can take a major toll on you and your family. Sharing it with them, however, can only strengthen your bond and help everyone navigate the journey ahead."

When family members are secretive about important matters, the secret itself may become irrelevant while the fact that information was withheld takes on greater meaning. It's natural to feel conflicted about communicating the details of sad or horrific events. Therapists agree, however, that the lack of communication or secrecy can cause emotional damage to both children and adults. When the truth is finally recognized by daughters, healing can begin.

This was true for sixty-nine-year-old Maureen who I spoke with over the phone. Her story demonstrates how damage can result when there is secrecy and a lack of communication within a family system.

Maureen's Teenage Loss Story

"I was eighteen years old and a college student when my mother died of breast cancer at the age of forty-six. My three siblings and I didn't even know my mother had a mastectomy. Part of what made my mother's death so difficult was that we didn't even know she was sick, much less dying, until the last few weeks of her life.

"Cancer was never talked about in my family. My mother died two or three weeks after we found out she had cancer. The suddenness of her death was very difficult. I was overwhelmingly sad and felt a sense of great loss for many, many years. Because of the secrecy, the delayed information, and the lack of communication following my mother's sudden death, I didn't begin to feel really whole until my thirties and beyond. The worst part of it all was that my family, myself included, never said a word about my mother's death after the initial period of informing everyone. If I'd talked about my mother and her death early on, I would not have felt so alone and sad for so many years."

Maureen cried as she recounted the heartbreaking scenario of the last weeks before her mother died. "My mother died at home and I remember every detail of her last days. The last week of her life she lived in a chaise lounge in the dining room. My twelve-year-old brother didn't really know what was going on.

"My father didn't talk about mom after she died and didn't display any photos of her. It felt like he was saying that her death was an everyday event and we were expected to go on with our lives. I felt an emptiness for many years. It was hard to go on sometimes. However, death made me more empathetic to the sorrows of others and eventually gave me strength. Later, as I experienced trials in my life I would think, *I got through losing my mother, what could be worse?*

"My advice is, if you get sick, tell your children. Get help if you need it. If you don't talk about your loss, your pain will seek other avenues. I hope my story will make a difference for those who might be tempted to keep secrets or those who are recovering from living in a secret-keeping family."

Maya Angelou writes, "There is no agony like bearing an untold story inside you." This sentiment echoes Maureen's experience. Having the opportunity to process a mother's illness and death not only helps a daughter move forward with her healing process, it also establishes a model for handling difficulties throughout her life. Daughters who grow up with unresolved secrets may repeat the secret-keeping scenario as they face additional challenges.

Although my dad and I had an open dialogue about my mother after she died, I rarely talked about my mother's death, or the fact I didn't have a mother, with people outside of our tiny family circle. As with other early loss daughters with whom I spoke, I didn't want to be in a position to have to admit to my peers that I was motherless. If the topic of family came up in a group of my young friends, I would find an excuse to leave the circle. If I had no choice but to speak, I was honest and told them my mother had died. I believe this hesitancy to talk about my experience was a result of not wanting to appear different or less-than because

I had no mother. The lack of communication, even with my best childhood friend, Jenny, is an example.

Growing up, Jenny and I were very close. We walked to school together, she was practically a second daughter to my dad, and we frequently had sleepovers where we shared our hopes and dreams, such as joining the newly formed Peace Corps. Even though we saw each other every day at school, we talked on the phone for hours when we returned home.

Jenny had a long, dark brown ponytail, lovely brown eyes, and three younger brothers. She was a straight-A student who excelled in journalism. Although Jenny and I went to the same college, we grew apart our freshman year due to living in different dorms, pledging different sororities, and establishing new friendships. Jenny has lived in North Carolina much of her adult life, while I resided in Illinois. We did stay in touch through Christmas cards and the occasional class reunions.

Remembering that Jenny's mom died when we were in college, I called her for an interview when I began work on this book. Early in our conversation, we were both surprised to realize how little we knew about the death of each other's mothers. I couldn't even remember what year her mother had died and she'd forgotten that I was only eight when I lost mine.

When we spoke, we simultaneously exclaimed, "How could we have been so close for so many years and never discussed our mothers' deaths?"

Jenny's mother, a gentle, dark-haired woman who I remember well, died at age forty-six, the summer after Jenny's freshman year in college. Jenny recalled that I attended her mother's funeral but I have no recollection of being there. Her mother died of breast cancer. Two or three years before her death, she had both breasts removed and, at the time of her death, she was being treated at the Mayo Clinic.

Jenny's Teenage Loss Story

"I clearly remember getting the call from my dad, who had accompanied my mom to Minneapolis, telling me my mother had died. I was at home for the summer helping to take care of my three younger brothers ages ten, fourteen, and seventeen. Jimmy, the ten-year-old, was the only one home at the time and after I hung up the phone and shared the tragic and unexpected news with him, we locked ourselves in our tiny bathroom and cried for a long time."

One month later, Jenny returned to college, picking up her activities and studies where she had left off, not talking to anyone about her mother's death. "I think college was an escape for me. Also, my dad was a very traditional '60s dad and I was afraid he would want me to quit school, come home, and take care of my brothers. Thankfully, this never happened. I think he knew how important my mom considered college to be. She had also attended Hastings College but only for one year as her dad thought it wasn't important for a girl to be educated. She wanted more for me. Perhaps knowing her wishes, my dad left me in college and figured out how to raise my three younger brothers on his own."

Guilt associated with her mother loss has also played a part in Jenny's life over the years. "Looking back, I feel guilty that I wasn't there to help my family more during the summers before my mother died. I was determined to be on my own, have a job, and make my own money. To their credit, my parents never said, 'Stay home, we need you,' but later I realized they did need me and I regret not being there for them."

I've examined what might have kept Jenny and I from discussing our common mother loss experience and I have no plausible explanation other than, for me, life had moved on. As I explained earlier, I didn't speak of my mother loss as a child or teenager. By the time Jenny's mother died, we had drifted apart and no longer had heart to heart discussions. Even if this wasn't the case, it seems like carrying on "the secret life of a motherless daughter" was the norm for both of us. I regret that I didn't call Jenny earlier and offer to talk to her about our common loss.

We were especially grateful, however, that finally, after fifty years, we were having a bonding mother loss conversation. We discovered that it is never too late to open up the secrecy trap and share your mother loss experience with a trusted friend. It was a special moment for both of us.

Early loss daughters like Jenny and I are not the only ones who rarely speak of their loss. Daughters who have mothers with dementia frequently experience the negative result of secret-keeping as well.

"Dementia is such a secret disease," wrote Crystal, a caregiver for her mother and a daughter I met on the Dementia and Alzheimer's Support Group on Facebook. "I keep finding out that friends of mine had parents with the disease but they were silent until their loved one passed. I hate that we are all so alone in this stupid life."

Recovering from the feelings of guilt and the circumstances of secrecy can be challenging. In my experience, and the experience of daughters with whom I spoke, maturity and distance from the trauma, brings healing and the likelihood of more open dialogue. As we become adults and move into middle age and beyond, not having a mother is less unusual. A motherless adult is less the object of pity than a motherless child.

Frequently, self-sufficiency and confidence begin to surface as we move forward. Today, being a daughter of early loss is part of who I am. I now recognize that the independence I developed as a result of being motherless helped me blossom into a person with vital self-esteem. Like the daughters with whom I spoke, I too want to take my story out of the closet in order to make a difference in the lives of others. With time, we can move beyond the need to hide the reality of our lives.

Henri Nouwen, Dutch Catholic priest and professor, taught at a variety of academic institutions including the University of Notre Dame, Yale Divinity School and Harvard Divinity School. Later, Nouwen worked with mentally and physically handicapped people at the L'Arche Daybreak community in Richmond Hill, Ontario. Nouwen sums up by calling all of us "wounded healers."

Nobody escapes being wounded. We are all wounded people, whether physically, emotionally, mentally, or spiritually. The main question is not, 'How can we hide our wounds?' so we don't have to be embarrassed, but 'How can we put our woundedness in the service of others?' When our wounds cease to be a source of shame, and become a source of healing, we have become Wounded Healers.

Now What?

As you consider Step Five, extract yourself from the guilt and secrecy traps if you find yourself in them. Work on accepting that it's not the fault of the daughter how the adults around her handled loss. Look at your present and evaluate your relationship with guilt and secrecy.

Coaching Questions

- What secrets are a part of your family's history?

- How does secret-keeping impact you and your efforts to move forward?

- If you are experiencing guilt over the loss of your mother or the circumstances of her death, what can you do to move away from this feeling? With whom might you speak to help you move forward?

BE ALERT TO ABANDONMENT FEARS AND THE DARK SIDE

*Abandonment doesn't have the sharp but
dissipating sting of a slap. It's like a punch
to the gut, bruising your skin and driving
the precious air from your body.*

—Tayari Jones, author

The fear of abandonment is a common and reoccurring theme in the lives of early loss daughters and, of course, daughters who were physically or emotionally abandoned. Children may expand the meaning of a traumatic life experience to be universal. For instance, a daughter might say to herself, *My mother died and left me so others will also die and leave me.*

As an adult, our core beliefs about how the world works can be built on these limited, and possibly, untrue assumptions. This may cause us to to form beliefs such as: The world is a dangerous place, I don't deserve to be loved, there is no safe place for me, or I'm destined to be alone.

Mary Ann is an early loss daughter who had a fear of abandonment. We were connected through a mutual acquaintance and spoke twice on the phone.

Mary Ann's Early Loss Story

"I was ten when my mother died of heart failure on Mother's Day. She was forty-nine. I will be turning fifty soon and I'm quite aware that I will have lived longer than she did. I have two older brothers. My father raised us by himself. My dad wasn't a great communicator but he did his best. He had dinner on the table every night at six o'clock. He didn't want anyone to feel sorry for us. He wanted us to move forward with our lives. However, I missed the nurturing aspect of my mother.

"Although I was a straight-A student, my high school years were horrible. I was bullied and rejected to such an extent that I had to change schools. I felt that I had been rejected by my mom when she died, then rejected by my classmates. After some hard times, I learned that nothing good comes from rummaging in the past.

"I've never married or had children. It took me fifty years to connect the dots and realize I am afraid of abandonment. My father never remarried and he was loyal to my mom even after she died. My father and I became very connected. Over the years, I also became attached to my brothers. I felt like we were the last ones on the lifeboat. To me, family relationships are sacred.

"Today, I'm (finally) in a long-term relationship with a man I've known since I was sixteen. We plan to buy a house together. I think I'm figuring things out and learning to override my abandonment fears."

Mary Ann wanted to share the following advice with other daughters living with abandonment issues. "Let gratitude strengthen you. Although losing my mother was the defining moment of my life, I've learned to give the event its place and kick out my feelings of abandonment."

Like Mary Ann, the fear of abandonment has been a significant issue in my life as well. It showed up originally when my mom was still alive and I feared being left behind as my family made preparations to go out of town for her medical care. Later, it manifested in how anxious I felt when my dad was late returning home from work. I was fortunate, however, to have a dad who understood the need to provide me with an ultra-secure environment in order to help me fend off my fears. He did this by turning down promotions so we didn't have to move and he didn't date or frequently leave home other than to go to work. I learned to trust my relationship with him and I began to feel that my life was secure. When I was young, however, I did have a contingency plan for my future in case something happened to my dad. Since I didn't want to be raised by either of my aunts, my plan was I'd run away if my dad died. My plan lacked specific details but the fact I had a plan seemed to calm my fears.

As an adult, the fear of abandonment first showed up in my marriage. This is how it manifested. One summer day, my first husband, Jim, was supposed to pick up our four-year-old daughter, Katie, from pre-school. He forgot. When he finally showed up, she was sitting on the curb in front of the park district building that housed her pre-school. He had always been the "Absentminded Professor" type, even as a young adult. I had overlooked this absentmindedness for several years, but on this day I let go of my "never fight /just overlook" resolve which, I now realize, partially manifested from my own fear of abandonment.

There is nothing like a mother's fury when the safety of her child is at stake. I called him irresponsible. In hindsight, I should have qualified it as irresponsible in this instance because, in all other ways, he was a very responsible, caring person. But, I'm sure I just said, "You are irresponsible!" His response? He didn't speak to me for an entire weekend, a weekend spent on a family camping trip.

If he had denied my accusation with words—even loud, angry words—the impact for me would have been significant but brief. His silence, which I unknowingly translated as abandonment, was devastating. This was a reality I figured out much later while in therapy. To be fair, I should have told him how extremely anxious his silence made me feel. At the time, however, I wasn't that mature and I knew little about how to confront appropriately. As a result, our communication began to break down. At the time, I wasn't aware the communication issue was connected to my deepseated fear of abandonment.

I do believe that his silence was so frightening I never wanted to experience it again. Had I not been a motherless daughter, I believe my reaction would have been less dramatic. After that incident I don't recall angrily confronting my husband again on any major issue for fear I would, once again, feel abandoned. Over time, the result was resentment. Those unexpressed negative feelings compounded into unspoken large and small objections, criticisms, and a host of other negative feelings—a toxic mix for a marriage.

In my experience, the fear of abandonment led to the fear of confrontation. I learned that the inability to confront in a healthy way is a common malady among the motherless daughters with whom I spoke. As I researched this issue, I came across the following helpful advice from Melissa Eisler, Certified Leadership and Career Coach and author. Eisler wrote:

Before you even dive into confrontation, there is some preparation work you can do that will help you weigh the risks and build confidence and clarity around your goals.

1. Assess Risks - What do you stand to lose if you confront? What do you stand to lose if you don't? Are your fears realistic?

2. Assess Goals - If you are secretly entering into a confrontation hoping that things will magically be set right—that you will be supported and nurtured the way you want or have always longed for—you may be highly disappointed during your confrontation. Recognize and relinquish any and all unrealistic expectations you are carrying, to the greatest extent possible.

3. Make a Plan - Make sure you know what you are standing up for and prepare to clearly express that objective. A plan will help you make clear and concise points and to be confident.

4. Meditate - Sit with your thoughts, discomforts, and fears and allow yourself to organize your thoughts and define objectives.

5. Learn From the Past - Reflect on what worked well and what did not in past confrontations. This can help you find areas you can improve and areas you want to repeat.

Many motherless daughters who fear abandonment and confrontation are so accustomed to remaining silent that "letting things go" feels like the only safe and normal path. That's how it felt for me. It wasn't until I encountered negative results from my lack of confrontation that I finally realized I had internal work to do. I wish Melissa's advice had been available to me forty years ago.

Not only is it important to learn how to confront other people, at times we must also look inside and confront ourselves. Unlocking truths about our mothers beyond remembering her as ideal or "practically perfect" or as an "evil and uncaring person" may require internal work. Revelations of the complete and complicated person she was may contradict what we've invented over the years to keep our relationship either positive and our mother "perfect" or remembering the relationship to be only miserable and unforgivable. It's important to reconcile ourselves to the truth in order to move forward and develop healthy self-esteem. If all we remember of our mothers is perfection, how can we possibly live up to her image? How can we accept ourselves, warts and all, if our role model is a perfect person?

Peg Streep, author of *Daughter Detox: Recovering from an Unloving Mother and Reclaiming Your Life*, writes, "The taboos about dissing our mothers, and the myths of motherhood which portray all mothers as loving, serve to isolate unloved daughters."

In an attempt to free unloved daughters or daughters with less than desirable mother relationships, I want to address the darker side of my mother memories.

As I read through my past writing in preparation for this book, I realized that now is not the first time I have thought of this darker side of my mother and our brief relationship. As I recounted earlier, upon turning fifty, I recalled as many memories of my mother as I could and made an effort to be honest in my remembrances.

As I look back on my mother's personality from an adult perspective, I believe in many ways she didn't have a chance to fully mature. She was only three when her mother died. From the stories I was told by my dad, my mother's Aunt Eugenia, the single aunt who moved in to care for the three motherless girls, was very strict and showed little love. For instance, my dad told me Aunt Eugenia insisted he call my mother Winnifred, never Winnie, when they were dating. She always wore purple. Although the color wasn't black, in my mind wearing purple feels like a person in constant mourning.

My cousin recently shared that her mother told her that our grandfather felt responsible for his wife's untimely death and threw himself into his work as a way of coping with his grief. I'm wondering what impact this might have had on my mother's early development especially if, prior to becoming a widower, he had been more available to her.

If my assumptions are correct and my mother didn't receive the love and support she needed growing up, I'm wondering how capable she was of fully loving a daughter. This comes to mind because, sadly, my memories of her don't include affection. My dad, aunts, and my mother's friends frequently told me that my mother loved me dearly.

However, I have no memories of her hugging me, reading to me, caressing me, or demonstrating signs of affection. This doesn't mean she didn't—I hope and, from the stories of others, believe she did—but I have no memories on which to draw.

Perhaps not remembering endearments is how I have protected myself from the sad feelings of loss. In researching this concept, I discovered Janie Perez's article, *3 Easy Ways to Stay Optimistic*. In it she writes, "Our brains are hardwired to prioritize bad, difficult, or painful thoughts over positive ones. Making matters worse, negative events quickly lodge themselves in our long-term memories, whereas happy memories require dedicated thought—twelve seconds or more—just to have a shot at landing in our memory banks for the long haul."

Continuing along this line, Rick Hanson, Ph.D., Senior Fellow of University of California Berkeley's Greater Good Science Center writes:

> Negative stimuli produce more neural activity than do equally intense positive ones. From an evolutionary standpoint, our ancestors' predisposition to Debbie Downer-ism makes sense. Ancient humans lacked reliable sources of food, water and shelter, and, as a result, made life-or-death decisions more frequently than we do today. To keep our ancestors alive, Mother Nature evolved a brain that routinely tricked them into making three mistakes: overestimating threats, underestimating opportunities, and underestimating resources. This is a great way to pass on gene copies but a lousy way to promote quality of life.

So, perhaps it isn't surprising that I remember the time my mother called me in to dinner and, as she closed the front door, I stuck my tongue out thinking she couldn't see me. I wanted to stay outside and was mad at her for calling me in. Unfortunately, she was looking through the peephole. She opened the door, snatched me up, and gave me a severe talking to. This is a very precise, vivid memory. It's even an endearing one because, through my adult eyes, I see it as her caring about me and my behavior. It seems to be an indicator that she wanted me to grow up to be a respectful person.

After much thought and meditation, I believe I have exhausted my memory bank of both positive and negative memories from the eight short years I had with my mother. Even though I have no distinct, loving memories, I have concluded that my mother loved me and I feel satisfied.

As part of my Croning Ceremony, I wrote the following poem that recalled my mom-memories. It was the first time I openly admitted my lack of love memories and the "dark side" of my mother loss story.

Pink Carnations
Bridge parties with forget-me-not flowered china on linen covered card tables,
Sunday mornings reading the funnies….three in a bed,
Coffee klatches in the morning sun and freedom from responsibility.

But love, where was the love?
Were your hugs and kisses forgotten or non-existent?
Did you regret my birth, the difficult labor in a far off, lonely place, the dirty lace curtains flying in the window.

No longer the precious little sister and Daddy's Darling,
But now a woman, a wife, a mother.
I was your treasure, a mirror image of yourself.
But, perhaps you were still the motherless daughter stuck in childhood.

Oh, how I wish I could have seen you dance!
The beautiful girl, full of music and rhythm, love and laughter.

Did the pink carnations suit you?
A girlish color, my favorite.
Your spark is a part of me still.
The spark I rarely saw or felt has become an everlasting flame.

And now, another.
The same eyes, smile, and zest for life.
Pink carnations are on the table.

This honest reflection of my feelings was an important step forward in my journey.

Bethany, an adopted daughter who was referred to me by a mutual friend, was also willing to uncover the darker side of her history. She hungered to learn the story of how and why she was put up for adoption. She was also curious to learn about the circumstances of her conception. We spoke over the phone.

Bethany's Adoption Story

"I was adopted as a baby. When I turned eighteen, I wanted to meet the lady whose tummy I was in so I connected with my birth mother through the aunt who had arranged my adoption. I learned that she was sixteen and a Mormon when I was born. I was sad when I discovered that she felt guilty her whole life about giving me up. I reassured her that she did the right thing."

The darker side of Bethany's life included never feeling connected to her adoptive mother. "My adopted mother was able to take six weeks off of work for maternity leave after I arrived. So, I had six weeks with her before she returned to work. Then she dropped me off with a baby sitter who I eventually thought of as my Soul Mom. She was my primary caregiver during the day until I reached school age."

Bethany always wondered, *Where do I fit in?* "I actually had three moms; a Biological Mom, an Adopted Mom, and a Soul Mom. My Soul Mom was special because she and I bonded from the beginning. I attached to her more than I did to my Adopted Mom. My Soul Mom was calm, loving, and emotionally stable. She loved me unconditionally and provided me with the security I needed.

"When I lost my Soul Mom last year, I realized how pivotal she'd been in my life. I owe a lot of who I am to her. She was light and love. I think she embodied what I think a mother ought to be."

Now, at thirty-four, Bethany is finding peace with who she is. "Coming to terms with my past and discovering who I am, has been a very challenging experience. I had to figure out how to navigate the relationship with my adoptive parents and my biological family. I'm constantly looking at the nature versus nurture debate in my experience on this planet." As Bethany uncovered the darker, shadow side of her life, she took steps toward greater personal understanding.

In addition to not knowing the complete, early story, sometimes the lack of communication about a mother when a father quickly remarries brings on dark feelings. This was true for Tami whom I met through a mutual friend. When we spoke over the phone, Tami told me her dad remarried six months after her mother died.

Tami's Early Loss Story

"Even though I was only six when my mother died, my father's remarrying felt sudden. Despite this, my dad and I were close. The difficult part of my relationship with him, besides the fact he quickly married someone who I felt didn't understand me, was he never talked about my mother. It was like she had disappeared.

"My darker side was that I felt very angry at my mother for dying. I went so far as to wonder if I was adopted. It seemed to be the only explanation I could conceive of that explained why she was willing to leave me. I even felt she had left me on purpose. I felt this way because, after surviving one round of breast cancer treatment and remission, when the cancer returned, my mother chose to not resume treatment. I thought she had given up, that she didn't love me enough to try. I wish I would have understood then, as a six-year-old and beyond, what I know now at fifty-five. My mother wasn't trying to leave me or giving up, she wanted to be present for me in the time she had left.

"The anger toward my mother became a chip on my shoulder. Then, when my stepmother also died of cancer, my father told me this story. 'Because I was with both your mother and stepmother at the end, I could tell when their faces relaxed and they were no longer in pain, that they were gone.' "

As Tami tearfully related this story to me she said, "This is when I stopped being really mad. This is when I finally realized how much suffering my mother had endured, why she didn't want it to continue, and why she thought being there for me without the drama of treatment was for the best."

Tami moved out of the darkness of her perception into the light of reality.

As I've aged, I've also learned the importance of embracing the full range of my feelings as I remember my history. This includes anger. It took me many years to realize that it's healthy to feel angry about some of my life experiences. Allowing yourself to feel anger, even if it's toward your dead mother, may be healthy for you as well.

Perhaps you are angry with your mother for leaving you or for causing you to drop your life as you knew it and become her caregiver. You may be angry that she didn't take care of herself, which you believe contributed to her death.

Feeling anger toward the people who didn't support you or care for you properly after your mother's death is also normal. Maybe you're angry with God for allowing terrible things to happen in your life. You may even be angry with your friends who are currently enjoying their mothers, doing all the things with them that you'd like to be doing with your mom. It's common to be angry or, at least, disappointed with family members who shirked their responsibilities when it was time to help care for their aging mother.

After you acknowledge your anger, and, if appropriate, confront those who acted irresponsibly, consider finding forgiveness for those individuals. Perhaps if you look beyond the behavior that caused your anger and search for the reason, you can give yourself the gift of forgiveness and move forward.

Another daughter who needed to shed some light on the reality of her mother and their relationship was Nicole. Speaking with her over the phone, I learned Nicole is a thirty-three-year-old, freelance writer.

Nicole's Early Loss Story

"My mother was diagnosed with lymphoma about the time I was born. She refused chemotherapy treatment because she wanted to breast feed me, which she did. Her cancer then went into remission for the next ten years. Of course, at the time, I had no idea about this cancer crisis. Then, when I was ten, my mom's cancer returned and she told me she was sick. A friend's mom had died of cancer so I knew it was something very bad. My mom assured me by saying, 'I'm going to do my very, very best to get well.' Unfortunately, she started to drift away and died when I was twelve."

Nicole has two older brothers; an autistic brother who is nine years older and another brother who is five years older. Together with their father, the four made their way in the world, but Nicole kept her mom close to her heart.

"My mom was the best mom in the world. She was incredible. I was so lucky to have her. She was a breath of fresh air, a nurse, a mom who filled our house with animals and was very involved in our lives. I've had her on a pedestal my whole life. I know I need to see all aspects of my mom, including the negative, but I still beat myself up when I'm not perfect like I perceive her to have been."

In her book, *Mothers and Daughters: Loving and Letting Go,* author Evelyn Bassoff addresses daughters like Nicole. "One of the marks of a mature relationship occurs when the daughter no longer sees her mother as goddess, monster or fool, but rather a human being."

Nicole, who recently attended a Motherless Daughters retreat led by author, Hope Edelman, knows she must move beyond this idealization.

"I think part of why I'm a bit stuck is because of the age I was when my mother died. Twelve was a challenging age to lose a mother. I was just starting to come into my own. I had gotten my period a year before my mom died and had the usual insecurities of a pre-teen wondering who I was and what my beliefs were. I feel like I've dealt with many mother loss issues, including the issue of abandonment, then something crops up and I wonder, *What would my mom do?"*

As we concluded our conversation, Nicole shared this lovely image. "When I was in second grade, my teacher tore a red, paper heart in two to demonstrate what it was like for our classmates when we said bad things about them. She then taped the two pieces back together to demonstrate how the hurt we caused can be repaired but it will never be exactly the same. I feel this is what it's like to lose a mother. The grief and feeling of loss does get better, but life will never be the same."

But what about those daughters who can't remember when their hearts were torn apart or put back together? Do daughters of very early loss experience feelings of abandonment or see a dark side to their mother? If one has never known the love of a mother, does she experience loss the same way? Addressing this question in her book, *The Loss That Is Forever,* author Maxine Harris, PhD, writes, "Loss requires some prior relationship. One can experience emptiness, however, when one has known only absence. For the survivors of the very early death of a parent, emptiness and void are inextricably tied with the enigmatic image of a parent they never knew."

Harris goes on to explain that all deaths are not created equal. "Some are sudden, violent or unexpected. Untimely death shatters our assumptions about how the world works."

My experience supports Harris' words. Even if we experience the death of a pet or distant relative, as young children, we are oblivious to the long-term impact of death. With a little maturity, however, we can realize that our experience shattered our assumptions about how the world works.

Children who experience a catastrophic loss, learn early that people do die, life does end, and tragedy can strike at any moment. These premature lessons for a child can feel like being immersed in the dark side of life if they aren't handled with love and understanding. Overcoming the fear of abandonment can be a lifelong journey. Recognizing this potential fear and being willing to examine it's roots are part of Step Six. It's important to learn that we can survive "leavings" without feeling abandoned. As adults, we are now able to take care of ourselves and survive. As we build a history of more people remaining in our lives than leaving, the strangle-hold of abandonment will lessen and, perhaps, fade away.

Then, let's face it, not all mothers are loving, nurturing, Hallmark card women. Yet, it's often difficult to be realistic about our mothers because the taboos around being negative are so pervasive. With maturity, we come to realize that every human being, even our beloved mothers, is imperfect.

Embracing and understanding these imperfections will help us shed the weight we carry from the dark side of our mother loss story.

Now What?

As you work on Step Six, ask friends and relatives to tell you their truths about the person your mother was—encourage them to be completely honest. As the picture of your mother moves closer to reality, you will find it easier to accept yourself and your future. Be prepared to deal with abandonment issues from time to time and know that these feelings are not unusual for daughters of early loss.

Coaching Questions

- If you have experienced unrealistic feelings of abandonment, how and when have they shown up in your life? How did you deal with these feelings? Have you had any success moving past your feelings of abandonment? How might you deal with them in the future?

- If you think you're repressing anything about your relationship with your mother, consider what that might be. Write down whatever comes to mind. Let it flow.

- What were your mother's less-than-perfect traits? How can acknowledging these traits make a difference in how you accept yourself and others?

STEP SEVEN

TAKE CARE OF YOURSELF

*We get well so we can become
our best self and help the world.*

—Sarah Wilson, journalist

Do you think regular exercise, getting a full night's sleep, healthy eating, paying attention to spirituality/faith or taking time out to be alone are selfish or self-indulgent objectives? Before we examine Step Seven, let's reframe self-care.

Rather than a selfish act, I challenge you to think of self-care as a path to being the best at what you want to do and who you want to be in the world. To be a great parent, colleague, spouse, caregiver, friend—you need to practice good self-care. To break out of a cycle of depression, anxiety, or negative thinking—you need to practice good self-care. An Indian spiritual leader put it this way. It's about watering the root so you can enjoy the fruit. In other words, it's important to keep our bodies, minds, and souls, our roots, healthy so we can bear fruit, make a difference, and live our best life. Self-care is also one more important step in your "Now What?" process.

Laura understood the importance of practicing self-care in all aspects of her life but admitted to backsliding in recent years and suffering the consequences. Laura, age forty-nine at the time we spoke over the phone, was abandoned by her mother when she was a baby.

Laura's Abandonment Story

"When I was eighteen months old, my mother left our family and moved far away to New York to live and work with a guru and become part of an ashram, a spiritual hermitage. From what I've gathered from my dad, my mom had a troubled relationship with her mother and being a mom was just too much for her. Plus, she was sort of a 1970's hippie."

Laura's mother visited her once a year. When she was older, Laura confronted her mother about leaving the way she did but there was never closure and they never bonded.

"My dad remarried when I was two-and-a-half and I bonded somewhat with my stepmother who had mother issues of her own. We also fought a lot because I wanted her to make up for everything I had lost when my mother left.

"When I was twenty-six, my stepmother died and I experienced terrible grief. I think I was actually grieving the loss of both mothers. I became depressed, sought therapy, and took medication. Later, I became a social worker because I wanted to help others as I'd been helped."

Although Laura gained understanding about her past life, she still experiences anxiety, which she believes is a result of not being nurtured by her mother when she was very young. As I researched Laura's belief about early loss, I learned that many child psychologists believe that when a mother abandons a daughter younger than five or six, the daughter may have no memory of the actual leaving and have no choice but to accept what she is told. The cause of the mother leaving may never be addressed by her caregivers and, even more frequently, her grief and loss aren't acknowledged.

Unlike death, where there is much empathy and the expectation of sadness, the family often sweeps the consequences of abandonment under the carpet. This action can leave a daughter in emotional limbo and cause psychological issues as she grows up.

"I have always felt I wasn't good enough or smart enough," Laura continued. "I have intimacy issues along with anxiety. When I married and had children I thought to myself, *If I have a family, maybe all my negative feelings and anxiety will go away.* Of course, they didn't. I have two daughters, ages eight and fourteen. I feel driven to be 'the perfect parent' because I want to repair something within me. As a result, I over-focus on my kids. I have a constant fear of losing them. I overreact to anything that happens and consider the 'what-ifs' way too much."

In addition to her parenting, Laura also feels the emotional impact of being abandoned by her mother at a young age affected her marriage. "Sadly, I'm not sure we are going to make it. Also, at one time I found comfort and meaning in religion, which my neighbor, who became an understanding mentor, introduced into my life. I have even left this behind. In the past, I took better care of myself and worked on my issues in therapy. I know I need to get back to this good self-care for the sake of myself, my daughters, and my marriage."

I contacted Laura several months after our conversation to see what she was doing about self-care. Here's what she wrote:

"I'm still struggling with work, kids, and finding time for me. However, each day I take baby steps towards caring for my needs." When I asked her what baby steps she was taking she gave me her list. "I'm reading and listening to podcasts to help me grow mentally and spiritually, I hired a life coach for a few months, I'm trying to be more aware of my thoughts and what I believe to be true or untrue while getting rid of the negative self-talk. I'm also meditating when I can and I bought a kayak to help me take care of my body with exercise that is fun."

I congratulated Laura on her recent progress of caring for her mental, physical, and spiritual health.

If you are feeling depressed or, like Laura, you're experiencing anxiety, taking care of your physical body with exercise is particularly important. "For some people it works as well as antidepressants, although exercise alone isn't enough for someone with severe depression," says Dr. Michael Craig Miller, assistant professor of psychiatry at Harvard Medical School on the web site helpguide.org.

To be specific, according to recent studies done at the Harvard T.H. Chan School of Public Health, running for fifteen minutes a day or walking for an hour reduces the risk of major depression by twenty-six percent. Exercise reduces depression and, similarly, anxiety, because it promotes changes in the brain including neural growth, reduced inflammation, and new activity patterns that promote feelings of calm and well-being. Perhaps you already know about endorphins, those powerful chemicals in your brain that make you feel good. Exercise can also serve as a distraction and provide quiet time to help you break out of the cycle of negative thinking that often feeds depression and anxiety.

Right now you may be saying to yourself, *I'm tired, I have no energy, my body aches and the last thing I want to do right now is exercise. How do I flip the switch to begin?* Dr. Miller agrees that it's a hard cycle to break. "Start with five minutes a day of walking or any activity you enjoy," advises Dr. Miller. "Soon, five minutes of activity will become 10, and 10 will become 15. The key is to make it something you like and something that you'll want to keep doing." Other experts agree. If you make a concerted effort to exercise regularly, you should begin to feel better within a few weeks and, the more vigorous the activity, the faster your recovery.

As you take care of yourself through physical exercise, keep in mind that the creative activities we discussed in Step Four will also nurture your mind and are a part of your overall self-care.

Although my interviews with daughters who talked about the importance of nurturing their spirits practiced a Christian faith, other types of spiritual practices or faiths can also help a daughter move forward as she cares for this aspect of herself.

Faith played an important role in Sandy's life as she moved forward after losing her fifty-two-year-old mother to breast cancer when Sandy was twenty-six. Sandy and I once attended the same church and we renewed our friendship as we spoke on the phone.

Sandy's Young Adult Loss

"My mother had breast cancer for over three years. She had both breasts removed. I was her oldest child and already married when she died. My two younger brothers were in college.

"Although the weeks following my mother's death are a blur because so much was happening in my life including a move to another state, I do know that my faith helped me get through it all. I have spent my whole life in the church. The first thing we looked for after our move was a church home. This affiliation not only helped me adapt to a new neighborhood and make friends, it gave me a foundation of familiar ritual to rely upon as I grieved the loss of my mother."

When I learned that Sandy's husband of fifty-five years died recently, I communicated with her about this devastating loss. When we emailed, Sandy wrote that she trusts that her lifelong faith and the resilience she developed through her mother loss experience will sustain her through this new season of grief.

Another personal friend, Judy, also relied on her faith as she moved forward after the death of her mother. Judy was eight when her fifty-six-year-old mother died as a result of unsuccessful gall bladder surgery.

Judy's Early Loss Story

"I never knew my mom as a healthy mother. I only have one memory of my mom on crutches. Otherwise, I only remember her as a bedridden invalid. During this time, groups of people were always around. Church ladies came to visit and can food in the summer for our family to eat later. We lived on a farm but my dad also had a job in town.

"When I was five or six years old I started school in town. During the school year I lived at the pastor's house and went home on weekends. In the summer, I stayed at my older brother's house. In addition to the pastor and my older brother, I lived with a variety of relatives in about eight different places during my early childhood. Although I didn't have what would traditionally be considered a stable life, it was all I knew and I accepted my life as it was. I believe that the primary stability I had during this time came from our church family and my much older sisters who had left home by the time I started school.

"When I began junior high, I no longer stayed in town during the week. I lived with my dad and I took care of the house. My dad did the cooking. During this time, I had no one checking my homework or telling me I should do this or that."

Judy, seventy-two, married with two adult sons and grandchildren, is thankful for the difference her faith made in her topsy-turvy early life. "My faith is still the most important aspect of my life and I'm very grateful."

Self-care is one of the first aspects of life that can disappear when a daughter is caring for a mother with dementia. Libby's story illustrates the need for safeguarding your own life as you care for another's.

I met Libby though a support group for dementia caregivers on Facebook. Although I'm not a caregiver, I'm a member of this group to offer support to others. When we first talked on the phone, Libby admitted to feeling completely overwhelmed in her role as a full-time, at-home caregiver for her eighty-five-year-old mother who suffers from Alzheimer's.

Libby's Alzheimer's Loss Story

"My relationship with mom before her diagnosis was amazing. I couldn't have asked for a better friend, confidante, and teacher. We traveled to Hawaii, the Bahamas, and multiple day trips to casinos in Atlantic City. I trusted her with everything and frequently went to her for advice. She was a second mother to my son, not just a grandma.

"Even though my mom knows me about seventy-five percent of the time, I am devastated when she doesn't. Sometimes she says I don't look like 'her Libby' because I'm too old and my hair is different."

Libby has been her mother's part-time caregiver for two years and full-time caregiver for the past six months. Libby admits she is paying a big price.

"Although I'm there most of the time, when I am away, my mother tells the caregiver that I haven't been with her for days. It is so painful for me to hear. I only see my twenty-one-year-old son—who still lives at home—in passing and I've lost touch with ninety-nine percent of my friends. They have given up asking me to do things with them because they know I'm stuck at Mom's.

"In addition to losing contact with my friends, my relationship with my boyfriend is strained—to say the least. We have no privacy or time to be together. He comes and sits with me at Mom's but he's beginning to feel caged-in like I do. I feel like I'm in prison. I miss my life, my son, my boyfriend, and my friends. I miss normalcy!" Like many caregivers, Libby is sacrificing self-care and much of her personal life to be her mother's caregiver.

Just after Libby told me her story, her mother suffered a severe stroke and Libby called me with an update. "My mother signed a do-not-resuscitate order and I'm honoring it. When I worked in a hospital as a Licensed Practical Nurse, I frequently saw families who, even though there was a DNR, refused to let their loved ones go. I knew that I would follow my mother's wishes and allow her to die with dignity. I didn't call 911 when I knew she was having a stroke. I did call our hospice contact.

"Today we are in the final stages of my mom's life and yet, yesterday, Mom and I were out for a walk. It's hard to believe she is dying so suddenly. My sister is afraid to see death. My brother is not accepting the inevitability of her dying. I think my training and experience as a nurse prepared me for this moment."

I asked Libby what was next for her. "First I will have to learn how to live without my mom. She was my best friend. Then I will need to find my way back to my relationships and caring for myself. I'm prepared for what will happen in the next few days of my mother's life but I'm uncertain about my future."

Within a day of our last phone conversation, Libby emailed me to say her mother had died. Because I was concerned about Libby's well-being, I checked in with her several months later. Although she is feeling somewhat stuck in her grief, Libby is taking better care of herself. She's going to the gym, watching her diet, and quit smoking. She also tapped into her creative side and is enjoying making stained glass projects with a friend. Sadly, she and her boyfriend broke up.

Even though Libby admits to having a difficult time right now, she's confident that she'll get through this period of her life. "Let your readers know that they may never be completely okay but they will find different ways to cope and move forward." As Libby recovers from her time as a caregiver and mourns the death of her beloved mother, I hope she puts herself in the forefront and embraces Step Seven.

Experts in the field acknowledge that the gradual losses experienced by caregivers can lead to sadness, depression, anger, guilt, sleeplessness, and other physical and emotional problems. According to the web site aging-care.com, statistics show that at least thirty percent of caregivers die before those they are caring for. Caregivers are as important as the people they care for. If they abuse their bodies, minds and spirits while caring for others, no one wins. Good self-care is critical if the caregiver is to survive in her role.

My sixty-eight-year-old friend, "Jennifer," a caregiver for her ninety-year-old mother who has dementia, reinforced this message.

"I've survived three divorces and I've been sober for twenty-four years. None of these challenges were as difficult as having a mother with dementia even though she is in assisted living. When I was discussing this situation with my AA sponsor she gave me this good advice. 'It isn't your responsibility to help your mother lengthen her life at the expense of shortening yours.' I'm taking this advice to heart by renewing my commitment to good self-care."

Sometimes good self-care means learning how to come to terms with the anger a daughter has toward a mother who wasn't present or nurturing during her early life. Finding wholeness again can be challenging.

After experiencing life as an angry person, Carol found her way forward by renewing her spiritual life. Carol and I met through a mutual friend and she emailed me her story. Carol didn't lose her mother through death or total abandonment but her mother was frequently absent and her mother's uncaring behavior negatively impacted Carol for many years. It wasn't until she was a teenager that she came to realize that alcoholism was involved in how her mother behaved.

Carol's Partial Abandonment Story

My mother moved out of our house when I was two months old. Although, my father and his family helped raise me and my two older brothers, we were the Ragamuffin Kids who had no regular supervision, no clean clothes, no hot meals, and our home was a mess. I stayed at my grandparents' house on Friday nights and my grandmother fixed my hair. Most of the responsibility for my care fell to my brothers. They were stuck with me all of the time. Dad worked full-time and at night he was dating to 'find a mother' for us.

As a result of these early years, I consciously looked for a man to marry who was self-sufficient and could take care of me. However, after I found the person who met my criteria, I became the controlling caretaker of everything. I wanted to create the 'perfect' family.

Carol described herself as a very co-dependent mother, getting her own identity from her children.

I wanted to do and give everything to my kids that my parents didn't give to us. It hit me when my son was born just how helpless I was when my mother left. I saw the selfish act more clearly and became even more bitter and resentful.

I didn't think she deserved to be involved with her grand-children. I was a mean, angry, and self-righteous bully. I had no empathy, sympathy, or tolerance for weakness. I thought I deserved to be angry because of my mother's choices. As a result, I learned to manipulate others to get what I wanted or needed. I learned to do things myself as I thought no one could do it as good as I could. I frequently felt better when I pointed out the mistakes of others. I was a compassionless person.

After many years as a "compassionless person," Carol returned to the faith of her youth and began to change her life.

As a child, I was introduced to Jesus, but I didn't have a personal faith. As an older adult, I finally turned my life around when I truly recognized Christ as my Lord and Savior. This relationship changed me. I want to tell daughters who have difficult relationships that they are not alone. Trust in God to fill the empty place in your heart. No person can fill this hole—not stuff, not your husband, not your children.

Everything has a purpose and we are made to glorify our Creator. We can find joy even in unfavorable circum-stances. We have free will to choose anger and resent-ment, loneliness and low self-esteem or faith, strength, joy and purpose in our lives.

By taking care of her spiritual side, Carol turned her anger around and found the joy she'd been seeking for many years.

Wayne Dyer, philosopher, self-help author, and motivational speaker, had an experience similar to Carol's. He writes, "One of the greatest lessons of my own life was learning to turn the inner rampage of hatred and anger toward my own father for his reprehensible behavior and abandonment of his family into an inner reaction more closely aligned with God and God-realized love."

I learned early the value of nurturing my spiritual connection. My faith journey began when I was eight years old. Although I regularly attended Sunday school, I'd only prayed rote prayers like, *Now I Lay Me Down to Sleep*. Intuiting the dire circumstances surrounding my mother's illness, I prayed my first personal, heart-felt prayer when my mother was in the hospital. As I held the paper pill cups she'd given me, I prayed, *Dear God, please help my mom get better real soon. Amen.*

Those early prayers were the beginning of my personal relationship with God. Although my prayers weren't answered in the way I'd hoped, I didn't come away angry. Conversely, this beginning of a personal relationship with God was the foundation of a faith that continues today.

In addition to supporting me as I moved forward in my early years as a motherless child, my faith also helped me to take care of myself later when Keith, my husband of ten months, died suddenly of a heart attack. At his memorial service, I found myself standing in front of a few hundred people. I hadn't planned on speaking, but there I was at the lectern saying, "Keith was a rock in my life and I will miss him terribly. But God is an even bigger rock. I know He is with me and He will see me through."

With this statement, I affirmed my faith and my future. As my daughters, who stayed with me in the early days after Keith's death, made sure I was eating and sleeping well, I took care of this spiritual side of my life as I had learned to do as an eight-year-old. During this time of shock and grief, I was able to once again call on God and trust Him to see me through.

At the time of our loss, we may feel spiritually abandoned and alone. Even Jesus, as he hung on the cross, wondered for a moment where God was in his suffering saying, "My God, my God, why have you forsaken me?" (Mark 15:33-34) I believe everyone has moments when they feel forsaken. As we shake our fist at God in our anger or disappointment, I believe even these expressions are acts of faith.

Taking care of our minds and bodies through good nutrition is also beneficial and has been proven to reduce the symptoms of depression and anxiety. The following information was taken from an article by Rachael Schultz on the web site healthline.com.

"Changing your nutrition can be a great addition to traditional therapy, like CBT (Cognitive Behavioral Therapy) and medication, [but it] comes at a much smaller cost and can be a great way to self-care," says Anika Knüppel, researcher and PhD student at University College London and contributor to the European MooDFOOD program which focuses on preventing depression through food. "There are two ways nutritional interventions can help mental health: by increasing healthy habits and reducing unhealthy ones. For the best outcome, you have to do both," says Knüppel.

Research has shown that the Mediterranean diet which emphasizes the importance of adding healthy fats, whole grains, legumes, and plenty of fresh fruit and vegetables is one of the best nutritional guidelines for healthy eating. In addition, many studies have found that simply reducing or eliminating sugar from the diet can be life-changing when it comes to symptoms of depression and anxiety.

From time to time, like most women, my focus has been on caring for others rather than caring for myself. However, I've always considered that being the first of three generations of women to live beyond my 30's was a special gift I needed to honor and cherish. This "gift of life after thirty" continues to motivate me to be a Gym Rat Grandma, a person who eats her fruits and veggies, and a woman who seeks out experiences of wonder and joy.

I don't claim to have all the answers when it comes to self care. I have lapses in my exercise program, I need to lose more-than-a-few pounds, at times I question aspects of my faith, and I frequently "veg out" on mindless social media, but I do understand the importance of good self-care throughout a lifetime.

Ghandi believed that religion—and I would add self-care in general— is a personal matter between each person and his Maker. He advised taking a lesson from the rose. "A rose does not need to preach. It simply spreads its fragrance. The fragrance is its own sermon." Be the rose as you spread your fragrance to others and show them (and yourself) how good self-care can smooth the path on the journey forward.

Now What?

How we take care of our physical, emotional, and spiritual well-being is very personal. However, I encourage you not to under estimate the importance of good self care! The hard truth of why we aren't doing what we know we need to do may need to be explored.

Coaching Questions

- If you believe that self-care like exercise, healthy eating, personal time, and engaging in a spiritual practice is selfish or optional, how might you reconsider this notion?

- What do you need to do to take better care of yourself? Be specific. What's keeping you from doing this?

- What's one thing you will change this week to become a healthier (in all ways), happier person? Baby steps count!

STEP EIGHT

EXAMINE YOUR RELATIONSHIP EXPECTATIONS

Nothing is perfect. Life is messy.
Relationships are complex. Outcomes
are uncertain. People are irrational.

—Hugh Mackay, psychologist and writer

Until I began interviewing daughters and asking them about their marriages and other close relationships, it didn't occur to me that mother loss could have a significant impact on this segment of our lives. As I observed comments by members of caregiver and mother loss Internet groups, I frequently read postings like, "My husband just doesn't understand why I'm not moving on. He says he's sick and tired of my moping around." Or, "My friends don't understand the emotional and physical energy I use taking care of my mother. They have given up on me as their friend."

One person whose story fit this pattern was Melie. We met in an Internet support group and she agreed to share her mother loss story with me over the phone. Melie was twenty-seven when her fifty-three-year-old mother died. Melie's father died when she was seven.

Melie's Young Adult Loss Story

"My mother died quickly from cancer. We found out her diagnosis in December and she was gone by March."

Melie believes that losing her mother affected most of her relationships. "My friends didn't understand why I wasn't over losing her and I believe that my grief came between us. I can easily become angry with my husband when he doesn't appreciate what his mother does for him or when he doesn't do enough for her.

"My daughters, ages thirteen and eighteen, were born after my mother died. I keep a close eye on their relationship with each other. When they argue, I make them talk it out with their knees touching. I tell them, 'Someday I won't be here and your sister will be the only person who remembers how crazy your mom was.' My heightened sense of mortality has influenced my relationship with them.

"My older sister and I weren't close until after our mother died. Now, she is the person I call when I have a problem. We have become mothers to each other."

As I talked with other daughters, it seemed that the death of their mothers either brought them closer to their siblings, like Melie, or caused them to pull apart. Rarely was the sibling relationship the same as it was before her death.

When we closely examine our relationships, we may find that our mother loss experience shaped more of our relationship choices than we previous considered. For example, perhaps we steer clear of making friends with older women, fearing they will precede us in death. Or, conversely, we unconsciously choose older women as friends in order to fill the hole the loss of our mother left in our hearts. We may want more appreciation, acknowledgement, or love from our friends or spouses than is realistic. Perhaps we find it difficult to get close to friends or family because we don't want to experience the pain of loss again.

Although it took me years to come to this truth, I can finally say that the early loss of my mother impacted my relationships as well—especially my marriages. I've been married three times. In 1991, I was divorced from my college sweetheart after twenty-five years of marriage. After being single for eight years, I remarried in 1999. My fifty-three-year-old husband died suddenly of a heart attack ten months later. In 2002, I married my current husband. Throughout these marriages, I had intimacy, abandonment, and confrontation issues, which, I believe, related in some way to my mother loss experience.

As a young woman, I had unrealistic expectations about marriage. I grew up hearing about how much my parents loved one another. My dad claimed he and my mother never fought. Perhaps I thought this was a benchmark for a successful marriage because I didn't want to fight or confront or argue or discuss negative feelings. In fact, not fighting and, subsequently, internalizing negative feelings was one of the pitfalls of my first marriage and has been problematic in relationships throughout my life. Because I so briefly saw my parent's marriage firsthand, I had no way to evaluate the truth of their relationship.

I had no close-up role models, no mentors or confidantes, when it came to marriage. Although I had friends whose parents were together, I generally only interacted with their moms. My dad and I had only one couple who were friends with both of us. I had no relatives living nearby. I had one grandmother, both of my grandfathers died when I was five.

Although I've been married to three caring, honest, God-loving, and faithful men, I've not always found marriage to be easy. My father and I had a non-sexual, totally appropriate relationship, but I grew up more as his partner than his daughter. For instance, I was aware of our family's finances, helped make decisions about vacations, and cooperated with meal planning and housekeeping. I sometimes wonder if this unusual relationship impacted my marital relationships.

I met my first husband when I was a college freshman and he was a college senior. I worked hard to graduate a semester early so we could be married as soon as possible. I completed practice teaching, graduated from college, organized a wedding, and moved to Georgia all in the month of December 1966.

Looking back, it seems strange that I didn't feel the extreme sadness of not having a mother during this life-changing month of my life. Perhaps it was because, by then, I'd grown accustomed to life without a mom. I shopped for my wedding dress, chose red satin dresses with white fur pillbox hats and muffs for my bridesmaids. I did this by myself without shedding a tear.

The Christmas wedding, held December 17, 1966, was a candlelight ceremony in a church dressed for the holidays. It was a beautiful wedding and fifty-two years later it is still a lovely memory. My beloved dad walked me down the aisle and I was mostly joyful with just a hint of trepidation.

Perhaps my mother would have asked me how I felt about marriage or talked to me about what it was like to be a wife.

In my experience, it was customary to wear a special outfit as you left town after the wedding and reception. Mine was a purple suit with matching purple heels and feather hat. I believe I subconsciously chose the color purple because it was the color of my mother's wedding attire. Today, as I'm more aware, the fact that we were dressed similarly is a fond memory and a connection to my mom.

After my divorce in 1991, I spent much of the next eight years acting like an irresponsible teenager thirty years after the fact. Thankfully, in 1996, I met Keith, a sweet, sensible guy who grew up in Kansas. We met through a personals ad. (This was before Internet dating!)

Keith and I were married October 2, 1999 with a turn-of-the-nineteenth-century themed wedding. I wore a nineteenth century replica dress and our wedding party arrived at the reception in vintage cars. Our wedding luncheon featured an old-fashion barbershop quartet.

Keith was a healthy guy who jogged, frequently worked out at the gym, and was two years my junior. Despite his apparent good health, on the evening of August 10, 2000, just ten months after our wedding, Keith dropped dead of a heart attack while working out at the gym. Teenagers who were serving as lifeguards at the adjoining swimming pool performed CPR prior to the ambulance arriving, but they couldn't revive him. Later, I reassured these distraught kids that they did all they could for Keith. He was only fifty-three-years-old.

The evening he died, I was participating in a small group at a location unfamiliar to my children so no one was able to track me down (this was before the wide-use of cell phones.) When I returned home, about 8:30 pm, my neighbor, Joanne, came to my house to tell me Keith was in the hospital and she would drive me there. When the receptionist ushered me into a small room at the hospital, I was greeted by all three of my grown children, my pastor, my ex-husband, his wife, and a doctor. I knew immediately something catastrophic had happened.

I have no doubt that my mother loss experience gave me the tools to recover from both a heart-wrenching divorce, and then eight years later, the sudden death of my new husband. I had learned early that bad things can and do happen and relationships can bring heartache. I also learned that friends and family members were sources of strength. Lastly, I knew that God would comfort and support me as I moved forward.

Losing a mom can sometimes mean changing or losing other significant relationships at the same time. This was true for Christina, whom I met online. When Christina's mother died, she not only lost her mother, she also lost her mother's family of origin and connection to her heritage. We spoke on the phone.

Christina's Early Loss Story

"Few people know this about me, but I frequently feel lonely and awkward when I'm around women who are speaking about their amazing families and the support they receive from their relatives. It sounds so foreign to me.

"My mom, who died at forty when I was ten, was an only child and born in Japan. When she passed away, we lost all interaction with the Japanese side of my family. According to my dad and others, this schism was due to language barriers and them not knowing how to deal with their pain. I not only lost my mom but also her family—all at the same time. Losing all of these significant relationships and my cultural connection was very difficult for me.

"My dad was a good man with a good heart but a broken soul. He had a drinking problem and no clue how to step up to being a single parent. He tried to fill his emotional void with either alcohol or women in the form of multiple marriages. I longed for mom-type support."

Like many daughters of early loss, Christina also had difficulties with her marriage relationships.

"I don't really speak of this, but I'm in my fourth marriage. Not having a positive marriage role model affected my relationship choices. It wasn't until I sought therapy in my early thirties, that I learned to be present in my marriage and not flee when the tough times hit.

"I have been married now for seven years and we're going strong. The big thing I learned in therapy was how deep-seated my fear of abandonment was and how much it impacted my marital relationships."

Now in her forties, Christina is still working on perspective. "I lost a sense of myself in those early years. I'm very productive and work hard but there is this little bit of self-doubt in the back of my mind about who I am."

While some daughters, like Christina, found marriage difficult, others discovered marriage to be the key to their resilience and happiness. This was true for eighty-one-year-old Marion, whom I spoke with on the phone. Marion was eleven when her forty-five-year-old mother died. Married over fifty-eight years, Marion considers herself fortunate to have found a good man.

Marion's Early Loss Story

"I married right out of high school at age eighteen. I went from living with my father to my husband. Being the youngest of three motherless daughters, I learned early to do Mom Jobs like cleaning and cooking. Even though I was young when we married, I was prepared to be a wife. My oldest sister helped me with my babies.

"I was fortunate to have had a terrific husband. I inherited a temper from my mother but my husband helped me to calm down. He gave me stability and was wonderful with our children. For instance, he put a swimming pool and an ice rink in the backyard because he wanted them close by.

"Perhaps because I grew up without a mom, I tended to be too lenient with my children but my husband helped to balance me out." For Marion, her loving relationship with her husband was the anchor through the ups and downs of life, which included losing a daughter.

Marion's daughter died from vasculitis when she was fifty-one years old. Marion introduced me to her granddaughter, Lauren, who was thirteen when her mother died. I spoke with Lauren over the phone.

Lauren's Teenage Loss Story

"My mom was constantly in and out of the hospital and sick all of my life. Until I was in middle school, I thought this was normal. My mother also had seizures and passed out a lot. Even though my mother spoiled me because I was her only child, I had to grow up fast. After she died, I had to parent my father due to his drinking. We moved away from our family connections, which made it even more difficult. Those relationships had sustained me.

"I'm not married, but I have a boyfriend. He is my rock. I've learned to keep my head up and that time does heal. I try to stay positive. Like my grandmother, I've learned that relationships matter."

For women like Marion and her granddaughter, Lauren, relationships added the dimension of love, stability, and balance they missed growing up without a mother.

Not only the death of a mother but the caregiving the daughter gives her mother prior to her mother's death can significantly impact close relationships. This was true for Pauline and her husband, Peter, who immigrated to the United States from Middlesbrough, England, in 1991. I met Pauline through a local writers' group. She is the author of nine books including, *If You Love Me, Kill Me*, a fictionalized account of her experiences taking care of her elderly mother who suffered from dementia. I spoke with Pauline personally.

Pauline's Alzheimer's Loss Story

"Five years after we emigrated, my husband and I became American citizens. We then petitioned for our daughter, her husband, and their four children to immigrate to America. Shortly after they joined us, we brought my eighty-three-year-old parents into the fold. It was difficult having ten people living in a three-bedroom, two-bathroom house. It was particularly overwhelming for my husband who became very negative. I also found the chaos difficult but rejoiced in having my family together again after being away for so long.

"After a few months, my daughter and her family moved to their own apartment leaving us to look after my parents. Peter and I were both weary of being caregivers. It was difficult to deal with Peter's pervasive negativity and our relationship became strained and distant. Things got worse after my father died and my mother's health deteriorated. Peter was especially angry and felt left out of my life because I was so tired from seeing to the needs of my mother."

Knowing that they are still married years later, I asked Pauline what they did to ease the issues in their relationship.

"We sought some marital counseling, but the biggest help came from a friend in England. I phoned her to vent and complain. She told me my mother was my greatest spiritual teacher and I should honor her as such. This advice totally changed my perspective on the situation. I was able to put the anger to one side and switched to gratitude that she was helping me in my spiritual life. Peter and I both respected Vicky's wisdom and took on board what she had to say."

This change of attitude was quite dramatic since Pauline had a history of a difficult mother relationship.

"I didn't really love my mother when we brought her from England. When I was a child and teenager, she neglected me emotionally and discounted me, leaving me with emotional scars. Yet, when I was caring for her, I grew to love her for her strength and vulnerability. However, taking care of my mother for seven years was a difficult task that left me empty, sucked dry of energy and life. It took a long time to recover, but I've absolutely no regrets."

The ebb and flow of relationships can be challenging under any circumstances. Balancing caregiving, work, and relationships requires patience, acceptance, and flexibility. As Pauline and others discovered, there are no good choices that satisfy everyone in these situations.

Relationship challenges may also include the mother who is receiving care. She may not clearly state her needs because she feels bad about imposing or she may feel so bitter about needing help that she becomes bossy. Some mothers express the full range of these feelings which is more confusing.

Abandonment issues, all-consuming caregiving, or unrealistic expectations can push relationships to the breaking point. Grief can also take a toll because it's primarily an individual experience. Empathetic partners may try to take on the burden but no one can totally understand another person's grief experience. I learned from daughters that grief can cause partners to become closer as they lean on one another for support or it can cause them to grow apart if the grieving daughter retreats into herself or her partner or other close relationships lose patience with the daughter's grief. Marital relationships may also suffer because the grieving partner does not want to experience physical intimacy at this time.

There are no ready or easy answers on how to ease relationship issues where mother loss is concerned. As in all relationships, asking for what you need as a grieving or caregiving daughter is extremely important. It's also important to exhibit patience with friends and family when they don't understand your grieving, abandonment, intimacy or other issues related to mother loss.

Now What?

Step Eight is designed to help you examine your relationship expectations and issues through the perspective of your mother loss experience. Make an effort to make sense of your feelings and actions then take responsibility for them as you move forward.

Coaching Questions

- In what way does your mother loss experience affect your relationships? Consider both the positive and negative impact. Be specific.

- Based on what you've learned about mother loss and relationships, how can you turn around the negativity you may be experiencing?

- What steps will you take to put this insight into action?

STEP NINE

SERVE OTHERS AS YOU EMBRACE HOPE, HUMOR, AND GRATITUDE

By showing up with hope to help others,
I'm guaranteed that hope is present. Then
my own hope increases. By creating hope
for others, I end up awash in the stuff.

—Anne Lamott, author

When we focus on our misfortunes, slights, guilts, trials, and tribulations, we step away from the flow of life. One way we can regain our vitality is to find ways to allow our energy to flow to others.

In *The Book of Joy*, the Dalai Lama writes about the flow of life and the secret to joy. He also addresses the truth that adversity, illness, and death are real and inevitable.

> We choose whether to add to these unavoidable facts of life with the suffering we create in our own minds and hearts, the chosen suffering. The more we make a different choice, to heal our own suffering, the more we can turn to others and help to address their suffering with

the laughter-filled, tear-stained eyes of the heart. And the more we turn away from our self-regard to wipe the tears from the eyes of another, the more—incredibly—we are able to bear, to heal, and to transcend our own suffering. This is the true secret to joy.

Sarah was a daughter who, early on, discovered how to transcend her own suffering by giving back as the Dalai Lama suggests. Detailed and deliberate, Sarah told me most of her mother loss story over the phone and emailed me the answers to follow up questions. Many months later, we met in person over lunch as we cultivated a friendship. Sarah was fourteen when her forty-three-year-old mother died of breast cancer.

Sarah's Teenage Loss Story

"Although my mother died at home, she technically didn't have hospice. She died in 1964 and the first modern hospice in the United Stated opened in 1974. Fortunately, my mom had a very forward-thinking doctor who allowed her to return home with morphine on demand. We had around the clock nurses so we really had hospice before its time without the follow up or bereavement component.

"Because of my mom dying at home, I didn't want to be there after her death so I went to school the day she died. My friend's dad called the school to let them know about my circumstances and my close friends protected me from prying questions. Prior to dying, my mom hired Mammy to be my caretaker. Mammy was my security and a critical person in my recovery. She stayed with me until her dying day, helping me take care of my children after I grew up. I'm thankful I had Mammy in my life. My dad was an alcoholic and too consumed with his own grief to be any kind of a meaningful parent."

Even though Mammy helped Sarah through her teen years and beyond, Sarah, now sixty-eight, still has what she calls "bubble-ups," questions about the early years after her mother died.

"My mom was a prominent person in town and had many friends. Sometimes I wonder where they were after she died. They certainly weren't there for me. The most difficult 'bubble-up' is when I think about all my mother has missed. She would have loved her grandkids. The thought just breaks my heart.

"After my mother died, I kind of floated through high school. I stayed out of trouble but I had no therapy or counseling. I went to college, hated it, and got married at twenty so I wouldn't have to go back to school or live with my alcoholic dad. It all made complete sense to me at the time. For the next ten years I settled down to married life and had three boys in four years. At the same time, I also served on boards and volunteered for the Humane Association, Family Services, our Community Foundation, the Art Center, and I sang in the church choir. Keeping busy was my therapy.

"My maternal grandfather died in 1972, his wife had a massive stroke three weeks later (I was her only relative so I took care of her until her death in 1976), and my dad died two months after my grandfather. Years later, I realized I never mourned any of them because I never made the time! That's when I started intensive therapy and worked on the issue of my mother's death as well."

As Sarah related the next part of her story, I could hear the joy and pride in her voice.

"I became involved with hospice in 1979. I eventually started a new hospice and kept it running for ten years. I was president and on the board of the Ohio Hospice Organization and in 2002, I received the National Hospice and Palliative Care Organization National Volunteer of the Year Award. I'm still volunteering and a board member of Hospice Care of Middletown. I think it's obvious that volunteering really helped me, although this is the first time I've thought about it that way.

"Early on I was taught that giving back is important so I never really considered the personal impact. During my divorce, when I threw myself even more into my hospice work, I did realize that life felt safer when I was volunteering. What could have been a better, more compassionate place for me to be? Besides my kids and grandkids, what I accomplished through hospice is what I'm proudest of."

Sarah is grateful for her years of volunteering. She felt that she learned early on in her life that she could regain her balance by helping others.

In addition to helping a daughter regain balance, volunteering can serve as a vehicle to fill the mother gap of an early loss daughter as it did for Roni. I introduced Roni in the first step of this book. Her mother, along with her mother's unborn child, died in an iron lung when Roni was eight.

Roni's Volunteer Story

"As a young woman, I frequently volunteered with older, mother-figure women. I found that having a maternal figure in my life was healing and gave me a sense of belonging. These women helped me fill my mother gap"

A life-long volunteer, Roni began serving others when she was in high school by helping prepare children for their first communions. "In my junior year, I was President of the Blessed Virgin Sodality, a group for women in my parish who did spiritual work. Later, after I was married and became a mother, I volunteered by overseeing many of my children's activities like school plays, Cub Scouts, and Girl Scouts. Doing this type of volunteer work helped me feel as though I was doing things I might have done with my mother had she survived.

"As an older person, I served as Board President and Executive Committee member of a homeless shelter, connecting with people who had hard lives, which were often precipitated by a loss. Most recently, I've volunteered at a summer camp for children who have lost a parent. Through this service, I've reconnected with the little girl still inside of me who understands the impact of parental loss. All of these volunteer activities have left me feeling empowered by the growth that was possible as a result of my early mother loss."

Like Roni and Sarah, volunteering also made a difference in my life. At fourteen, I was a Candy Striper in a Veteran's Hospital. I wrapped medical instruments to prepare them for the sterilizer, made hospital beds, and wrote letters for patients. As a teen, these experiences gave me a sense of accomplishment, responsibility, and the knowledge that I could make a difference in the lives of others. With the perspective of over sixty years, I believe my Candy Striper years also helped me keep an outward focus rather than an inward, "what about me?" attitude after losing my mother as a child.

While in college, I was a volunteer at Hope School, a day school for physically and mentally challenged children, and worked with patients in a mental hospital. As a young military wife, I was a Red Cross volunteer in a locked psychiatric ward in an Air Force hospital. I was pregnant with my first child at the time and the patients seemed to feel the need to take care of me rather than have me take care of them. For example, they shielded me from seeing new patients if they arrived in straight jackets.

As a young mother I was a Meals on Wheels volunteer, English language instructor, and tutor. As a businesswoman, I was Chair of the Board of Directors for a community mental health center and, later, the Board Chair for a dual campus continuing care organization for aging adults. More recently, I have been a tutor in Costa Rica and in my local school. I also work with an organization to identify young women for college scholarships and sing in a choir.

Serving ailing veterans and active servicemen gave me connection to my country. Helping to create policy for organizations that ministered to the elderly and mentally ill gave me connection to my local community. Volunteering with young people keeps me connected to the future. These are a few of the volunteer experiences dear to my heart. Giving back has always taken a central place in my life. Serving others has kept me focused outward, helping me move past my own losses or regrets.

Carrie, who I introduced in Step Two, recently discovered the benefits of giving back. Carrie was a caregiver for her mother who died as a result of Alzheimer's. As a teacher for the Deaf, I asked Carrie if working with her students helped her move forward after the death of her mother.

Carrie's Volunteer Story

"Yes, my students continually help me to move forward. They always make me laugh with their crazy comments. In addition, I recently had the opportunity to identify with and help a student whose mother passed away suddenly from a brain aneurysm. He and I had several conversations. We talked about how he felt he didn't have enough time with his mom and I told him I felt that way too even though I had much more time with my mom than he did with his. The experience gave me the opportunity to connect with some of my other students who have lost family members.

"Also, I've been thinking about going back to school to get a degree in social work. I could use the information to work with Deaf students but I could also work with senior citizens and their families. My mother loss experience made me want to help people going through what I went through with my mom having Alzheimer's, my time as a caregiver, and my eventual loss. I'm learning the value of reaching out to others."

As I reflected on the daughters who found solace in reaching out to others, I came across this beautiful quote by Janet Fitch. In her book, *White Oleander*, Fitch writes, "The pearls weren't really white, they were a warm oyster beige, with little knots in between so if they broke, you only lost one. I wished my life could be like that, knotted up so that even if something broke, the whole thing wouldn't come apart."

This quote illustrates what resilience means to me. A life knotted up so that even when the strand breaks, all the pearls of my life won't be lost. Serving others creates knots in my life. Other knots have the faces of friends and family on them. Even when the strand of my life breaks again, I will not lose all that is important to me.

In addition to putting knots between the pearls of my life, recognizing that the unexpected could be around the corner is also helpful. Years after the trauma of losing your mother, something out of the blue like a song or a smell may once again trigger tears or feelings of sadness. A pearl may, once again, slip off the thread of your life. There's no deadline on your feelings of grief—keep your pearls knotted.

Initially, when a daughter loses her mother, it's especially important to stay with the feelings of sadness, anger, or regret. On the other hand, it's important to not let those feelings be all consuming. Consciously shift your focus if you feel yourself falling into an abyss. Perhaps when you feel yourself falling, finding a way to serve others will help stop the downward slide.

Embracing Hope, Humor, and Gratitude

Tightly hugging hope to our chest is another way to help us move forward in our journey. Hope gives us the sense that things will work out. It's difficult to live without hope.

Confirming the importance of hope, Dr. Jerome Groopman writes the following in his book, *The Anatomy of Hope*: "Hope gives us the courage to confront our circumstances and the capacity to surmount them. For all my patients, hope, true hope, has proved as important as any medication I might prescribe or any procedure I might perform."

Just as a life preserver works in the water, hoping for a brighter, calmer, more joy-filled future can keep your head above the surface as you tread or gradually swim toward the

SERVE OTHERS AS YOU EMBRACE HOPE, HUMOR, AND GRATITUDE

shore. In addition to hope, humor and laughter can also help you move forward.

Author, Langston Hughes, writes, "Like a welcome summer rain, humor may suddenly cleanse and cool the earth, the air and you."

As I spoke with daughters, I noticed that sometimes they were caught off guard by the sound of their own laughter as they recalled humorous memories. At times women even apologized for their outward display of joy if they felt they were "supposed" to be in a period of grief. This saddens me, as I believe humor and laughter are great healers. In fact, laughter is so important to our physical and mental well-being that gelotologists (practitioners of gelotology, the study of laughter and its effects on the body) literally prescribe laughter as medicine. Dr. William Fry, MD, a gelotology pioneer and a Stanford University professor emeritus, experimented on himself as early as the 1960s. He drew blood samples while watching Laurel and Hardy movies and noted that laughter lowered blood pressure and enhanced immune-system function. A good laugh can also calm your stress response, boost your mood, and promote a greater sense of well-being.

Seek out humorous stories, movies, and friends. Humorist Erma Bombeck once wrote, "There is a thin line separating laughter and pain." Don't be afraid to cross that line because as laughter returns, we begin to heal.

Many daughters with whom I spoke expressed gratitude for having their mothers as long as they did, even if that time was short. They were also grateful to be alive themselves, particularly if they had surpassed the anniversary of their mother's death. Some, like myself, were grateful for their amazing father, grandmother, or other caretaker who stepped in and helped them regain their joy.

Daughters were grateful for having the opportunity to share in their mother's last moments. Daughters whose mothers suffered from dementia were grateful if they had one last glimpse of their former mother before she died. Every woman I spoke with was grateful for the opportunity to make a difference in the life of another daughter who had an experience similar to her own. Healing and peace begin with gratitude. I encourage you to make it a part of your journey.

Like hope, humor, and gratitude, dreaming and creating a vision for the future is another way to maintain the flow of your life. Dreaming, fueled by hope, is an act that visualizes the future. I dreamed of the day I'd be the first generation in three to live beyond my thirties and I dreamed of my daughters being present for their children as I envisioned them as parents. I currently dream of the day my grandchildren will grow to be loving, contributing adults.

After my husband died suddenly, I dreamed of becoming a Life Coach and how the realization of that dream would change my life and the lives of others in a positive way. Every dream begins with a dreamer—become that dreamer. Dream your best life then put in the time and energy to make it happen.

Sara Ban Breathnach, author of *Simple Abundance: A Day Book of Comfort and Joy*, writes, "There isn't one of us who doesn't still carry childhood wounds. Some are more horrific than others, but no matter how painful your young memories are, there were also glorious moments that kept you alive, or you would not be here today."

One way you can hold onto and tap into the "glorious moments" is by carrying on some of your mother's traditions. Perhaps you can bake her favorite Christmas cookies—I make my mom's Russian wedding cakes or "mice," as she called them. You might display her favorite painting, plant her special flowers, or wear her prized piece of jewelry.

Every day I wear a ring with two diamonds that belonged to both my mother and grandmother. It is my most precious possession. Seeing this ring reminds me of how grateful I am to have had a mom and for the opportunity to be a mom for over fifty years. When friends or strangers acknowledge my ring, it gives me the chance to share my story which helps me keep my connection to my mother and grandmother alive.

Carrying on your mother's traditions or showcasing her special possessions is also a way to share your memories of her with future generations. Even though your mother may not be there to bake cookies with her grandchildren, nieces, nephews, or godchildren, the tradition can continue.

Asking others to share their experience of your mother with you, whether she died young or old, is a way to create new memories. Since my own mother memories are limited, the remembrances of others carry extra weight. Because there are so few people left in the world who knew my mom, I'm incredibly grateful for even one new story.

In learning about my writing this book, Leanne, my friend since kindergarten, recently told me what she remembers from the day my mother died. I wasn't entirely surprised that she could recall this particular day sixty-five years in the past because Leanne has a memory like an elephant. Here's what she told me of her memory. "When I returned home from school the day your mother died, my mother had a tea towel over her head and was crying as she told me the sad and shocking news that your mom had died."

This short sentence is a precious gift to me. The memory not only reaffirms how much my mother was loved, it also says she continues to be remembered by others.

In addition to finding comfort in the memories of friends and relatives, you may also find solace in mother-like relationships. As a young girl I had strong negative feelings about people, other than my dad, who attempted to parent me. As an adult, however, I'm attracted to mother figures. Now, in my seventies, my best friends are frequently older, sweet, affectionate and, in a word, "motherly" women.

While most women hate being called "Honey" or "Sweetie" by their peers, I relish those terms of endearment when they are heartfelt and sincere. To me, they feel mother-like. I've found that no matter my age, filling that mother void brings me a sense of peace and fulfillment. In fact, I was recently inexplicably drawn to a woman I barely knew. Her name is Anne. Although she is a few years younger than I, she reminded me of what my mother might have looked like if she had lived into her seventies. I literally couldn't keep my eyes off of this brown-eyed woman with the sweet smile. I eventually told her why I was drawn to her and, as often happens, she too had a special mother-loss story to share. We've become close friends.

As we consider the complexities of Step Nine including giving to others, expressing gratitude, embracing hope, imbibing in humor, and shoring up our precious memories, the following poem seemed to be a summary of it all.

"Alive" by Winifred Mary Letts (1882-1972)

Because you live, though out of sight and reach,
I will, so help me God, live bravely too,
Taking the road with laughter and gay speech,
Alert, intent to give life all its due.
I will delight my soul with many things,
The humors of the street and books and plays,
Great rocks and waves winnowed by seagulls' wings,
Star-jeweled Winter nights, gold harvest days.

I will, for your sake, praise what I have missed,
The sweet content of long-united lives,
The sunrise joy of lovers who have kissed,
Children with flower-faces, happy wives.
And last, I will praise Death who gives anew
Brave life, adventurous love—and you.

Now What?

Love doesn't die, people do. As you give the love your
mother had for you and the love you had for your mother
(if this is true for you), to others, the love will come back to
you. Secure the pearls of your life with knots, live your life
with humor, hope, and a sense of gratitude and you will find
yourself moving forward.

Coaching questions

- How might reaching out to help others help you move forward in your mother loss journey?

- What are you truly grateful for right now?

- When was the last time you laughed out loud? How did laughing make you feel?

- What tradition, memory, or object of your mother's do you cherish and share with others?

STEP TEN

ACCEPT THE HAND YOU'RE DEALT

You either get bitter or you get better. It's that simple. You either take what has been dealt to you and allow it to make you a better person or you allow it to tear you down. The choice does not belong to fate. It belongs to YOU.

—Josh Shipp, youth motivational speaker

Actor Christopher Reeve once said, "You play the hand your dealt. I think the game's worthwhile." Considering his paralysis following a severe spinal cord injury, this quote carries much weight. As we consider Step Ten and learn to accept the hand we are dealt, we move beyond the pain of the past, begin to flourish in the present, and look forward to the future. We also model this important life lesson for others.

I have found that one way to accept the circumstances of life and begin to move past grief is to focus on the person who died or left. If the relationship was positive, consider what your mother meant to you, recall memories of lovely experiences, celebrate her contribution to the world. Even if your relationship was negative, consider what she missed and will miss in the future by removing herself from your life. With this focus, grief or acceptance will be easier than if you concentrate solely on yourself—what you've lost and how you're going to cope without your mother.

Susan Cain, author of *Quiet: The Power of Introverts in a World That Can't Stop Talking*, writes, "If you've interpreted the events of your life to mean that you're innately unlucky or unwise, then it's hard to look optimistically at the future. Conversely, if you acknowledge that you've made mistakes and faced difficulties but seek (or have already glimpsed) redemption, you'll feel a much greater sense of agency over your life (and your future)."

Theresa is an example of a daughter who learned to feel a sense of agency over her life and future and accepted the hand she was dealt. She emailed me the gist of her mother loss story in response to a request she received from a mutual acquaintance. We later talked in greater detail over the phone.

Theresa's Early Loss Story

"In 1972, I was nine years old and it was report card day when I came home from school and my mother told me my dad was sick. She said my aunt had taken him to the doctor so she could wait for me to return from school. Thirty minutes later my aunt called to say that my dad died of heart failure."

After relating this experience of losing her dad to a sudden death, Theresa continued by telling me her mother loss story.

"By July of 1974, just two years after my dad's untimely and sudden death, my mother was diagnosed with uterine cancer and also died. I was eleven. My sister, who was nineteen years older than I, unmarried, and lived twenty minutes away, turned her back on me and didn't take me in. As a consequence, my twenty-six-year-old brother and I had to figure out how to do life together without killing each other. My brother sacrificed a great deal for me. Granted, he had no patience, and still doesn't, but we laugh about it today.

"I would have been lost had it not been for my brother, the wives of his friends, and many others. I got so used to explaining to strangers why I had no parent representation at functions that it felt like a recording. We lived in a small town and many people knew our situation. Some would stare, some would offer to help, and some would just gossip. Between family and friends pulling together, we made it work and they got me raised—it took a village."

As a teenager, Theresa's Uncle Bob took her under his wing and helped her sort out her future.

"When I started high school, Uncle Bob told me to pick out where I wanted to go to college and he would send me. Unfortunately, after I started college, I was so homesick I nearly dropped out. My brother said, 'I'll come get you after you consider these two things. First, how you'll explain to Uncle Bob why you're blowing this opportunity. Second, talk to your sister about what it's like to work in a factory because that's all you'll be qualified to do.'

"Forty years later, I have a degree in social work and a successful career. I've never married and have no children primarily because I always think to myself, *What if I die on my child?* However, I'm in a relationship with a really good guy. And those wives of my brother's friends who played such a big role? I still text with them nearly every day."

Teresa went on to tell me that the wisdom she acquired from her life experiences included accepting the hand she was dealt.

"I believe you have to face reality, get on with your life, and accept what happened. I've never allowed myself to feel like a victim. I also try to live my life in a way that would make my mother proud. Her voice is in my head every morning saying, 'Make your bed.'"

C.S. Lewis, in his book *A Grief Observed*, likened accepting your life after mother loss to a man learning to walk after a leg has been amputated. Lewis writes, "The amputee may get along quite well, may even become facile and agile on crutches or on a carefully designed artificial limb. But the amputee must accommodate to permanent loss. He or she will never walk as before; repair does not mean a return to the way things were." In other words, the amputee must learn to play the hand she's dealt.

Those who experience the slow and painful mother loss associated with Alzheimer's, must also learn to accept their reality if they are to move forward.

"Kathy"—who asked that her real name not be used—was introduced to me by a memory care unit director. Kathy's mother was eighty-five and had lived in assisted living followed by memory care for the last two years. We spoke on the phone.

Kathy's Alzheimer's Loss Story

"At first we thought Mom's memory loss was simply age-related and nothing serious. Then she started receiving late notices on her bills and wasn't keeping up with her checkbook. In the past she had always been very meticulous about her financial matters. Next we discovered food left out to defrost had been on the counter all week.

"Before my mother had Alzheimer's, she was very outspoken and had a great deal of anxiety and fear. After the disease manifested, she became calmer, happier, less verbally abusive. Now she has less anxiety and fear. In fact, she doesn't have a worry in the world and is happy every day."

Kathy acknowledged that this change happened gradually.

"This didn't happen overnight. At first my mother wouldn't accept help of any kind. If we sent someone to her home to help her, she paid them and told them to go home. Now she is in a memory care unit. When I visit, I take her outside to the gardens or to a different dining room. She gets a kick out of my iPhone and thinks it's a toy."

Kathy learned early on that she had to let go of any embarrassment she felt in front of others and accept how her mother acted and looked. Some of Kathy's family members won't visit her mother because they are uncomfortable being around her.

"I think some of my family members are worried they could also have dementia in the future and seeing my mother is a reminder to them. Dealing with Alzheimer's can certainly damage family relationships. However, one thing that gives me comfort is knowing that my mom's heart and feelings are still in there. For instance, she recently saw her grandson with a cast on his arm and she got all emotional. She can no longer express herself in words but when she cries, I know she is still there.

"My advice to others is to be attuned to changes in your mother's lifestyle, don't be ashamed of what's happening, seek help, and learn to accept what is happening in your life as well as your mother's."

"Ashley"—who also asked that I not use her real name—emailed me a similar story. Like Kathy, she was comforted by signs showing her mother was "still in there." For Ashley, the sign was her mother's smile. However, it took Ashley's mother a long time to regain her smile.

Ashley's Alzheimer's Loss Story

My mother was diagnosed with dementia nine years ago. She had already stopped driving because she had a couple of very scary experiences getting lost in once familiar places. We didn't know about this until a few years later. At first, we suspected the multiple medications she was taking for fibromyalgia were causing her confusion. When a new doctor found no signs of the disease and took her off the medications, she became ill due to withdrawal. In fact, she missed my son's middle school graduation in 2010 because she was too sick to attend. She felt very bad about this, as her grandkids were very important to her.

As my mother's disease progressed, so did her anxiety. She often asked, 'Are people watching their kids out in the street? Where's Dad (meaning Ashley's dad)? How am I getting home? There's no Pepsi in the house because Dad doesn't like me drinking it.' She actually had Pepsi cans all over the house. Eventually these worries got broader and more constant. She was concerned about her own father's whereabouts. He had died many years earlier.

Mom started having panic attacks when I brought her to my house for lunch to give my dad some relief. She'd spent a great deal of time in this location and should have recognized it but even deep breathing, music, petting my dog, or walking didn't relieve the anxiety of being in, what she perceived to be, a strange location. She did love to garden and sometimes pulling weeds calmed her but during her last six months at home, she had no interest in anything.

When she started asking my dad to take her home and he told her this was her home, she got very mad. We didn't know how to handle it. The first time we told her that her parents had passed away a long time ago, we realized what a mistake we'd made. For her, it was like reliving their deaths all over again. We felt terrible. That's when we realized we had to live in her reality but it was hard not to make mistakes. It was especially difficult when she asked me, 'Are your parents still alive? Do I know them?'

Ashley and her family finally made the decision to move her mom into a memory care facility. "It was such a difficult decision. I was really stressed out the whole first year and had physical problems due to the stress. I have finally turned the corner and now accept what's happening and the necessity of her being there."

Not only has Ashley come to accept the necessity of her mom being in memory care, she now recognizes the benefits.

"Now, my mom and dad have quality time together. My dad and I are upset that strangers are bathing, dressing, and taking her to the toilet but we are comforted by her smile. Her anxiety is now gone, replaced by a lack of awareness. Although her speech has mostly disappeared, her smile still shines through."

It seems that even Ashley's mother has gotten to the stage of acceptance.

Accepting the hand you're dealt addresses many life events beyond mother loss. My daughter, Katie, now in her forties, wrote the following poem when she was a senior in high school. Through the poem, she demonstrated how she perceived my early mother loss as well as her own loss when her father and I divorced when she was fifteen. The poem is a snapshot of our family at the time she wrote it and even now, twenty some years later. She titles it "Winnie" for the grandmother she never knew.

"Winnie" by Katie Shrigley

I know that my mother loved her.
Her blood went bad and
The Craftsman lost her.
I never saw her,
Felt her.
She never got to teach my mother
'Bout training bras,
Bleeding days, or
How to be my MaMa.
She couldn't be here when we fell to pieces.
I was never a spoiled child.
Her blood knew I wasn't meant to be.
I know that she followed my mother,
Through corsages,
Make out sessions during Gun Smoke,
Labor times three,
The falling pieces…
She was here.
I never see her,

Touch her.
The three of us share this warm house.
I don't count her as "one,"
But Mother might.
We all share this house,
With our loud voices, flapping arms,
Crazy dancing, and
Crazy cooking.
She listens to us.
She couldn't get a word in edge wise
Even if her blood had worked.
My mother knows she's here.
She sees her in our hair,
Our eyes, and
Our outlandish femininity.
I never hear her,
See her.
The blood reaches us.
We are all we have.
The three of us…
We are what matters.

When Katie talks about the Craftsman, she may be referring to my dad who was an avid wood-lathe worker or the Craftsman could be God. The "falling to pieces" refers to my divorce.

I cry every time I read this. I'm not sure why. Perhaps it's because my daughter is putting herself in my place and thinking of what my mother and I missed. Mostly I think it's because I'm touched that my seventeen-year-old daughter thought of her childhood as "loud voices, flapping arms, crazy dancing and crazy cooking." That's how I want her to remember it. I don't want her, anymore than I want myself, to dwell on the loss of our family structure through divorce or scary feelings associated with the possibility of early death. To me, this poem exemplifies how we, as a family, accepted the good that came out of tragedy while staying in touch with reality. We accepted the hand we were dealt.

Now What?

As you begin to accept the hand you were dealt, you will discover the path back to joy, fulfillment, and contentedness. Along the way, check out who is in your corner. As you rediscover joy, it's important to have supportive people around you. Associate with friends and family members who will help you move in a positive direction. Also, get rid of the "shoulds" in your life. Do what you want to do, be who you want to be. Stop comparing yourself to others. Stop beating yourself up. Be kind and gentle with yourself.

Coaching Questions

- What's one thing you will do to begin to accept your mother loss experience?

- Acceptance doesn't mean embracing bad behavior on the part of others. In what ways can you accept past negative behavior and move on? How will this make a difference in your life?

- If there is someone holding you back from accepting the past, how will you keep from having them negatively influence you?

CONCLUSION

NEVER GIVE UP

Every ending is a beginning.
We just don't know it at the time.

—Mitch Albom, author

For those of you who feel vulnerable, alone, or sad, I want to encourage you to never give up and embrace hope as you move through your mother loss journey. Even those of us who lost our mothers many years ago, can be surprised by a new wave of sadness, experience renewed feelings of guilt, or relive our loss as we face our own mortality. I encourage all of us to have the motto, "Never Give Up."

Judi is a daughter who has lived her life with a "never give up" attitude. Judi's mother was physically present in her life but so emotionally detached Judi felt as though she was absent.

I met Judi in 1971 at a small church we both attended. We stayed in touch over the years and she contacted me when she found out about my book. She wanted to tell her story to make a difference in the lives of daughters whose mothers didn't die or leave them but were emotionally absent.

Judi's Emotionally Absent Mother Story

"You know, sometimes mothers are gone yet physically present. This was the case with my mom," Judi said as she recounted her past over lunch.

"I think the story of my mother's emotional rejection of me actually started with my maternal grandfather who was German and came through Ellis Island, New York, from a German sector of Russia. My mother was the last of five girls born into this family. My grandfather was desperate to have a son to carry on the name and, at last, my Uncle John was born following the birth of my mother. In this environment, I believe my mother felt 'less-than' for being born a girl. Likewise, I believe she regretted having me as her first born."

At the same time Judi was born, her mother's sister was delivering a prized son to the family. "From the beginning, my mother was emotionally absent. Even as young as four years old, I felt the need for outside validation because I wasn't getting it from my mother."

Later, to prove her worth, Judi felt she had to excel academically. "In addition to being a good student, I also felt I had to succeed with music and voice lessons as well as other aspects of my life. Although I tried to please my parents, they didn't even attend my voice recitals. My brother, on the other hand, who was always in trouble, held the position of my mother's favorite until the end of her life."

In addition to having an emotionally unavailable mother, Judi was sexually abused as a child and teenager by people outside of her family. Although Judi's brother took financial advantage of his mother, he remained her favorite and Judi continued to feel rejected by her mother until her mother's death. "This lifelong rejection is why I want to share my story. I believe my experiences demonstrate how painful mother loss can be even if a mother is still alive."

Despite her abusive and difficult childhood, Judi never gave up. She was resilient and determined to succeed and was the first in her family to go to college. When I asked Judi how she thought this was possible, she said, "I believe I had a compass inside that showed me how to make more of my life. I followed that compass and never gave up hope of where it would lead me."

My personal relationship with Judi confirms her self-assessment. When Judi and I met as young mothers, I considered her a mentor. She introduced me to *MS Magazine* and the importance of the Women's Movement. She was a successful career woman in the field of finance, a soloist in our church choir, and a loving wife and mother. Explaining her life as an adult, Judi said, "I learned what not to do from my parents. The last thing I wanted was to repeat their behavior."

Later in her life, Judi had an opportunity to once again tap into her desire to never give up. On March 11, 1997, Judi had a serious, life-altering stroke. After many months of rehabilitation, Judi made great physical progress, but still lacked confidence in who she had become after her stroke. To help her come out of isolation and regain a sense of self-confidence, Judi hired me as her Life Coach.

Although she no longer had a head for numbers, could not follow a recipe, or do other mental tasks she once did with ease, she eventually learned to accept herself and was proud of her recovery efforts. Judi came out of isolation and created a different, yet satisfying, life with her husband and two adult sons. She never gave up and was later able to say, "I've come to like the new me better than the old me. Finding my way through a life without a mother being emotionally present, gave me the tools to move forward through the ups and downs of my life. My advice to daughters is, no matter how lost they may feel, never give up. Push forward and keep your eye on the light at the end of the tunnel."

Maxine Harris, Ph.D. in her book *The Loss That is Forever*, shares the following metaphor, which I believe speaks to daughters, like Judi, who tackle difficulties and never give up.

> When a tree is struck by lightning, if it survives, its growth is altered. A knot may form where the lightning hit. The growth on one side of the tree may be more vigorous than on another side. The shape of the tree may change. An interesting twist or a curious split has replaced what might have otherwise been a straight line. The tree flourishes; it bears fruit, provides shade, becomes a home to birds and squirrels. It is not the same tree it would have been if there had not been a lightning storm; some say it is more interesting this way; few can even remember the event that changed its shape forever.

As a last mother loss story, I'm sharing Helen's and Jean's journey because their early life experiences, attitudes, and many decades of lives well-lived inspired me to never give up hope on life, love, and recovery.

I met Helen in church. We quickly became friends and she shared her abandonment, recovery, and adoption story with me. Jean, Helen's sister by adoption, also shared her story.

In 1945, Miss Wilhelmina Kalsbeek, the woman who eventually adopted both children, wrote Helen's and Jean's early stories for a missionary newsletter. I used some of the information from this first-hand account. I also spoke with Helen and Jean over a pot of tea at my dining room table. Throughout the story I use the names, Helen and Jean, names given to them by their adoptive mother. These daughters have no record of their birth names.

Jean's Early Abandonment Story

Jean was born in China in 1937, a year before the Japanese invasion. Jean's father was working away from home and her mother was very frightened to be living alone with an infant. When rumors emerged that the Japanese were quickly moving into the area, most of the young women fled the village. When a man urged Jean's mother to flee with him, she felt that doing so was a lesser evil than falling into the hands of the brutal Japanese soldiers. When she fled, she left her baby in the care of a hired wet nurse.

Wishing to also escape and avoid the enemy who was notorious for brutalizing women, the wet nurse took the baby to the child's maternal grandmother. The seventy-five-year-old woman protested that the child was not her responsibility but the wet nurse said that she could not be burdened with her.

The grandmother heard that her daughter had fled to Kuling, a village many miles away. Knowing she would lose her possessions, her home and, perhaps, her life to the enemy anyway, she decided to leave everything and make the trip with her granddaughter to try to find the baby's mother. Besides being elderly, the grandmother had tiny feet, which had once been bound. Despite these encumbrances, the grandmother reached the village of Kuling after walking for ten days.

When she arrived in the village, the grandmother told her story to everyone she met and inquired about her daughter. No one had heard of her. The grandmother and baby spent one more night outdoors in the yard that turned out to be the property of the mission where Miss Kalsbeek served. The next morning, Miss Kalsbeek and Ruby Liu, another missionary, found the old grandmother dead with the baby frantically sucking her breast. The missionaries took the baby to the hospital but, because she constantly cried, the ladies were asked to take her home with them.

Miss Kalsbeek wrote the following details in a newsletter:

This baby was the ugliest child we had ever seen! She had a big lopsided head and was covered in boils and sores. Her disposition was just as ugly. The only time she didn't cry was when she had a mouth full of food. We fed her nine times that first day as she was starving. She even wailed in her sleep. The day came when we thought we could no longer continue. We had other work to do and we were extremely tired and nervous. We prayed more than usual that day, asking for guidance. That night when we put the baby to bed, something unusual happened. She went to sleep and didn't cry. In fact, she slept like a perfectly normal child and from that day on she started to grow fatter, prettier, and sweeter. Apparently the Lord wanted us to keep her. She has been ours ever since.

As it turned out, taking care of little Jean was preparation for the arrival of Helen, the next, even greater, challenge.

Helen's Abandonment Story

When Helen was forty days old, her parents sent her to her future in-laws. In the Chinese tradition of arranged marriages, Helen was engaged before she was born. Her parents apparently rationalized that this baby would end up with her in-laws eventually so why not deliver her to them immediately so they could escape the Japanese invasion.

They arranged for their baby to travel with a man who they knew was going to the city where her future in-laws lived. By the time Helen was delivered to her future mother-in-law, she had been without adequate food for five days. Baby Helen arrived just as the family was packing to leave their home. Because the baby was a sacred trust, however, they felt compelled to bring her with them. Helen was given little food as the family traveled from village to village. When the family finally arrived in Kuling, they crowded into a tiny cottage with several other families. Annoyed by Helen's constant crying, the other families asked Helen's in-laws to leave the cottage.

Rather than lose their shelter, the family decided to leave the baby in a basket in the woods. After ten days, they returned to give her a proper burial, but found that she was still alive. On seeing her alive after so many days, they became frightened, believing that she must be a demon or a spirit child, and decided it would be too dangerous to kill her. They had heard about a mission and left the baby there.

Miss Kalsbeek picks up the story:

When we first uncovered the baby that was brought to us in a basket, we beheld the most pitiful sight we had ever seen. There was a note giving the baby's lunar birth date. She was three months old and weighed less than two and a half pounds. Ruby and I called in the doctor who, upon examination of the baby, said she couldn't possibly live more than a few more hours so we need not waste our time on her. Although the doctor had worked in a famine district, she said she had never seen a case this bad.

Because she had laid in urine for so long, the baby was raw from acid burn from her waist to her knees. She could not suck so we gave her a few drops of diluted milk from an eye dropper every little while. Her hands were like bird claws, her neck about the size of a skinny chicken. By nighttime, the baby was still alive so we fixed a bed for her. As we were carrying her through the room, we looked at her under the light. Just then, she opened her eyes and looked first at Ruby and then at me and smiled the sweetest smile we had ever seen. From that moment on, she held our hearts in her skinny little hands. For three weeks we watched over her night and day. In those early weeks, many villagers came to see our tiny baby. Each visitor invariably explained, 'She is even worse than I had heard!'

After three weeks, there was a change. At first it was gradual, then rapid. Believe it or not, that little mite of humanity developed into a lovely baby. Many folks came again to see her and called her the Miracle Child.

In 1949, at ages ten and eleven, Jean and Helen immigrated to Grand Rapids, Michigan along with Miss Ruby Liu, their Chinese foster grandmother, who they called

Mother. Grand Rapids was Miss Kalsbeek's original home. Soon after their arrival, Jean and Helen became U.S. citizens.

The girls attended a Christian elementary school, high school, and college. Helen later attended the University of Michigan on a scholarship and received a Master's Degree in Social Work. She worked in that field for almost forty years. Jean had an advanced Medical Technician degree and worked in pharmaceutical research. Jean and Helen are both married and they each have two sons.

Unlike the other motherless daughters I interviewed, Jean and Helen were raised by two "mothers," although it didn't feel that way to Helen. "I never felt like I had two mothers because we called Ruby Liu, the Chinese woman, Mother, and Miss Kalbeek, the American missionary woman, Granny, because she was older. In 1953, Granny legally adopted us because she was a United States citizen. Although she became our legal mother, we still always called her Granny."

Although Helen was abandoned twice, once by her mother and again by her future mother-in-law, she never had negative feelings about her early life. "All my life, I have only felt gratitude that I was adopted. Had it not been for Granny and Mother, I would have died. When asked about my medical history, I sometimes wonder about my biological parents and what they might have been like, but mostly I just feel a deep sense of gratitude for God's miracle in my life."

Although she once spoke fluent Chinese, Helen has since forgotten how to read her native language or speak it fluently. "When we went to live in Grand Rapids, we were surrounded by Caucasian people and were encouraged to speak English. I later married Sang Ki, a Korean, and we have always spoken English."

Summing up her life so far, Helen said, "As a Christian, I trust in God and I know that He loves me, cares for me, and leads me through difficult times. When we suffer setbacks, I believe it's important to find support through therapy, support groups, or the church. I believe in learning from the past but focusing on the future. If we never give up hope, I think every experience has the power to be a positive force in our lives. Helping others is also good therapy."

Jean, Helen, and their adoptive mothers never gave up—on life or each other.

Rare is the person who experiences a straight line, a smooth life, an uneventful existence. Though I would not wish the event of losing a mother on anyone, looking back, I see how developing meaningful life skills at an early age made, and continues to make, a difference in the quality of my life. I'm now at the age where my friends are dying. If I live long enough I will lose my good health, I've already lost my dear dad, and I may lose yet another husband. I have faith that the knots between the pearls of my life will hold and I will never give up hope.

A Word to Acknowledge Your Mother

As we conclude our time together I would like you to select a word that acknowledges your mother. Think of this word as a special stone or seashell from a treasured time or life experience. If you had a negative mother experience, you might have a negative word or perhaps your word is "grateful"—as in "I'm grateful that you birthed me."

I chose "smile" as my special memory word. My mother's smile was the gift she gave me that I pass on to others every day. The few people who remember my mother frequently comment on our similar smiles. I see it in her photos. I hope that her smile, passed on through me, brings a ray of light to others.

F. Scott Fitzgerald wrote, "We have two or three great moving experiences in our lives—experiences so great and moving that it doesn't seem at the time that anyone else has been caught up and pounded and dazzled and astonished and beaten and broken and rescued and illuminated and rewarded and humbled in just that way ever before."

Have the daughter stories in this book demonstrated that others have been "…beaten and broken and rescued and illuminated and rewarded and humbled" in ways that feel familiar to you? Do you feel less alone on this journey? Our mission isn't to ignore or hide or forget the fact of our mother loss. Our mission is to share our stories, remember our mothers and our experiences, be alert to consequences, be sad for our loss and glad for the love we experienced (if we did experience love), and grateful for what we've learned.

Now What?

As we take steps to move forward, let's remember that we aren't stepping away from our experience, we are taking it with us as we become the best of ourselves. We are stronger for our losses, braver for our sacrifices, and more loving in our empathy. We are the daughters of mother loss with the potential to be—strong, caring, resilient, mature, independent, empathetic women who never give up. This is what I want for you, Dear Reader.

Coaching Questions/Requests

- What aspect of your life today requires perseverance? What do you need to help you persevere and never give up?

- Consider the progress you've made since your mother loss experience. Remember how you once were, think about where you are today. Now, dream about where you want to be tomorrow.

- What will you be like in ten years? Visualize what you look like, what you're doing, who is in your life, and how you're feeling about yourself. In ten years, what will your mother loss experience mean to you?

ACKNOWLEDGEMENTS

*Remember there's no such thing as
a small act of kindness. Every act
creates a ripple with no logical end.*

—Scott Adams, creator of Dilbert

Thanks to Virginia Read who planted the seed for this book on a hot day in May, 2017 and introduced me to her Marco Island Writers Critique Group who guided me as I nurtured and watered that seed. A very special thanks to my editor, Elena Hartwell, who challenged and encouraged me with her professional expertise to write to the best of my ability. Thanks to my Beta readers Joy Martin, Mitch Bruski, Lois Colaprete, and Bob Alston for their insights and encouragement and to my proofreaders, Kristine Wruk and Linda Walker.

The work of Hope Edelman, the "mother" of motherless daughters, has inspired me and countless other motherless daughters for decades. Thanks, Hope, for blazing the trail. A special thanks to the women who shared their innermost feelings and memories as they told me their mother loss stories. I was constantly motivated to complete this book because I felt you behind me, encouraging me to share your stories in order to make a difference for others. This book is for you!

Sixty-six years ago my dad, Leon Horn, took up the reigns of being both mom and dad to a sad and bewildered eight-year-old girl. I could not have asked for a better parent. Thanks Dad, I love you!

SUGGESTED READING AND WORKS CITED

Alexander, Ty, *Things I Wish I Knew Before My Mother Died: Coping with Loss Every Day*, Mango, 2016

Alzheimer's Association web site: www.alz.org

Cain, Susan, *Quiet: The Power of Introverts in a World That Can't Stop Talking*, quietrev.com, Crown, 2012

Crossroads Hospice and Palliative Care: www.crossroadshospice.com

Edelman, Hope, *Motherless Daughters: The Legacy of Loss*, 20th Anniversary Edition, Da Capo Lifelong Books, 2014

From Both Sides of the Couch blog: www.andrearosenhaft.com

Gawande, Atul, *Being Mortal, Medicine and What Matters in the End*, Metropolitan Books, 2014

Harris, Maxine, *The Loss that is Forever; The Lifelong Impact of the Early Death of a Mother or Father*, Plume, 1995

Hayton, Pauline, *If You Love Me, Kill Me*, CreateSpace, 2013

His Holiness the Dalai Lama, Archbishop Desmond Tutu with Douglas Abrams, *The Book of Joy*, Penguin Random House, 2016

Idliby, Ranya, Oliver, Suzane, Warner, Pricilla, *The Faith Club, A Muslim, A Christian, A Jew—Three Women Search for*

Understanding, Free Press, A Division of Simon & Schuster, Inc, 2007

Imber-Black, Evan PhD, *The Secret Life of Families*, Bantam, 1999

Klass, Dennis, *Continuing Bonds: New Understandings of Grief*, Routledge, 1996

Kübler-Ross, Elizabeth, *On Death and Dying*, Scribner, 1969

Lowthert, Jenna Rose, *Life Still Goes On: The Blog Book of a Motherless Daughter*, Kindle book, 2017

Miller, Michael Craig, M.D. assistant professor of psychiatry at Harvard Medical School, www.helpguide.org

Myers, Linda Joy, *Don't Call Me Mother*, She Writes Press, 2013

Newman, Mildred & Berkowitz, Bernard, *How to Be Your Own Best Friend*, Ballantine Books, 1974

Schultz, Rachael, www.healthline.com

Taylor, Judy, *Mum Moments*, Positive Signs, 2014

The National Center for Victims of Crime (NCVC): www.victimsofcrime.org

Walker, Rozelle Jenee, M.D., *Good Night Beautiful Mother*, CreateSpace, 2017

White, Karen, *The Sound of Glass*, New American Library, 2015

YourHealthMatters, Dr. Nathan Hermann, www.health.sunnybrook.ca

ADDITIONAL
RESOURCES

A Box of Butterflies: Discovering the Unexpected Blessings All Around Us by Roma Downey

A Grace Disguised: How the Soul Grows Through Loss - Jerry L. Sittser

A Graceful Goodbye - A New Outlook On Death - Susan B. Mercer

A Mother's Reckoning - Living in the Aftermath of Tragedy - Sue Klebold

All Gone: A Memoir of My Mother's Dementia, With Refreshments - Alex Witchel

Always Too Soon - Book and website by Allison Gilbert

Becoming Myself: Living Life to the Fullest After Losing Your Parents - Shari Butler, PhD

Colors of Goodbye: A Memoir of Holding On, Letting Go, and Reclaiming Joy in the Wake of Loss - September Vaudrey

Dementia: Up Close and Personal: A Caregiver's Tale - Shirley Woolaway

Does Grief End? Turning the Corner After Mother's Death - article by Gemini Adams

EmpowerHER - www.empoweringher.org - Non-profit for daughters of mother loss up to age 24 including events, mentorship and virtual programming.

Feeding My Mother: Comfort and Laughter in the Kitchen as My Mom Lives with Memory Loss - Jann Aren

For *Millennials in Mourning, Grief Can Run Deep* - MPR Radio Program

Goodbye, Mama - Susan A. Lewis

Grieving a Parent's Death: A Different Goodbye for Millennials - article by Sammy Caiola

Grieving the Death of a Mother - Harold Ivan Smith

Helping Yourself Heal When a Parent Dies - article by Alan Wolfelt, PhD

Healing the Adult Child's Grieving Heart: 100 Practical Ideas After Your Parent Dies - Alan Wolfelt, PhD

How Losing a Mother Shapes the Parent You Become - Hope Edelman

How Millennials Mourn - article by Emily Kaiser

Hungry Hill - Carole O'Malley Gaunt

I Will Carry You - The Sacred Dance of Grief and Joy - audiobook by Angie Smith

I'm Still Smart: How Alzheimer's Took My Mom - Michael Lowry

In the Letting Go: Words to Heal the Heart on the Death of a Mother - Jonathon Lazear

Language Lessons (For When Your Mom Dies) - Mary Clare Griffin

Lessons on Loss: What Two Sisters Have Learned From Losing Their Mother to Cancer...So Far - article by Alexandra Detwiller and Anti Foster

Letters From Motherless Daughters, Hope Edelman

Losing a Parent: Passage to a New Way of Living - book and website by Alexandra Kennedy

Missing Mom - Joyce Carol Oates

Mom's Memory Was My 'Something Blue' - article by Marisa Renee Lee

Motherless Daughters Support Groups:
www.hopeedelman.com/support-groups

Mother Loss Workbook: Healing Exercises for Daughters workbook - Diane Hambrook

Never the Same: Coming to Terms with the Death of a Parent - Donna Schuurman

Old Life: A daughter's journey dealing with sudden loss - Christina Haines

One Woman's Journey: Recovering From Grief - Ruth Foreman

Parent Loss: Continuing Their Song - article by Marty Tousley

Something From Nothing: Getting Through My Grief - article by Karen Wyatt, MD

The Moment of Lift - Melinda Gates

Taking Time to Mourn a Mother's Death - article by Marty Tousley

The Dead Moms Club: A Memoir About Death, Grief, and Surviving the Mother of All Losses - Kate Spencer

The Dutch House - Ann Patchett

The Long Goodbye: A Memoir - Meghan O'Rourke

The Orphaned Adult: Understanding and Coping with Grief and Change after the Death of Our Parents - Alexander Levy

The Rainbow Comes and Goes: A Mother and Son On Life, Love, and Loss - Anderson Cooper and Gloria Vanderbilt

What Losing Your Mother Feels Like - Rachael Oakes-Ash

When Mom or Dad Dies: A Book for Comfort for Kids - Daniel Grippo

When Mom Dies: A Daughter's Unique Guide to Help Heal Grieving Hearts Today - Dackeyia Q. Sterling

When Breath Becomes Air - Paul Kalanithi

Wild: From Lost to Found on the Pacific Crest Trail - Cheryl Strayed

ABOUT
THE AUTHOR

MERSHON NIESNER has a background as a Certified Life Coach, child-welfare social worker, marketing/comm-unications entrepreneur, and a freelance writer. Her *Ask the Life Coach* column appears regularly in the *Coastal Breeze* newspaper. Mershon's blog, www.motherloss.blog, is followed by readers from around the world. She lives with her husband, Ken, on Marco Island, Florida. Between them they have six children, nineteen grandchildren, and eight great-grandchildren.

Thanks for reading. If you found this book meaningful, please consider leaving an honest review at your favorite book site.